"Finding God's will for one's life is always a question of paramount importance to everyone. Charles Specht in his book *Revealed* has answered that question. He shows not only why it is important, but exactly what the will of God for us is, and thus how to implement it in one's life. It is both a rebuke of the shallowness of contemporary Christianity and a great resource in discovering the revealed will of God for our lives. It is a great resource for all, and especially for the youth in our culture who are wrestling with the dilemma of finding God's expressed will for their lives. I highly recommend it as a must-read."

- ALEX D. MONTOYA
SENIOR PASTOR, FIRST FUNDAMENTAL BIBLE CHURCH
ASSOCIATE PROFESSOR, THE MASTER'S SEMINARY

"Everyone is seeking the answer to a common question—what does God want for my life? Charles Specht has written a book that helps everyone find the right conclusion to that God-sized question. *Revealed* is a journey of discovery of God's will and God's way. Read it, and buy one for a fellow traveler too!"

- BRANDON COX
PASTOR, GRACE HILLS CHURCH
EDITOR OF PASTORS.COM

"Charles has a fascinating way of bringing light to the truth. In an objective but incredibly direct fashion, he uses Scripture to raise a challenge to each and every one of us. *Revealed* is a fresh reminder of God's feelings toward us, and how our decision to follow Him should transform our soul."

- BRIAN GARDNER
CPO & PARTNER, COPYBLOGGER MEDIA, LLC
BLOGGER AT BRIANGARDNER.COM

"This book reads like a hot knife through butter because of the writer's engaging style, vivid illustrations, and soul-penetrating subject matter. Yet, serious readers will be stopped in their tracks constantly for self-evaluation. The result should be a jerk out of complacency and a jolt toward progressively growing in a passionate love of Christ, redeeming the time by filling life with worship, service, and witness following the will of God. I pray that many disciples will be made as a result of this work."

- BRIAN SHEALY
SENIOR PASTOR, FELLOWSHIP BIBLE CHURCH
FORMER ACADEMIC DEAN, THE CORNERSTONE SEMINARY

"I loved reading *Revealed*. It was well-written and engaging. However, what I love most about the book is its author. Charles lives what he has written. He is not writing from theory but from a genuine love for the Savior that is demonstrated in obedience to Him. Charles (his book too) is the real deal."

- DAVE PARKER
ASSOCIATE PASTOR, RIVERPARK BIBLE CHURCH

"*Revealed* provides a great insight into the Christian life. It is not about the mysterious will of God in the gray areas. It is about the absolute clear will of God provided in the Word of God. And God's will involves making disciples…which is why we still are inhaling and exhaling right now. The Lord left us here to do His will. His will is Great Commission Discipleship."

- GEORGE POSTHUMUS
SENIOR PASTOR, RIVERPARK BIBLE CHURCH

"*Revealed* thoroughly examines what it means to know and follow the will of God. Many Christians seem baffled regarding this topic that is so clearly and frequently laid out in the Scriptures. Specht helps remove the mystery in this area. He particularly stresses the will of God regarding discipleship and evangelism, which highlights a big focus of this book—following the will of God means obedience to the commands of Scripture, not necessarily fulfilling personal desires and goals."

- JOHN BULGER
FORMER SENIOR PASTOR, MENDON COMMUNITY CHURCH

"Charles Specht has in an interesting way reminded us of the riches of Scripture which have been revealed to guide us on our journey. This book will be useful for those seeking God's best in decision-making. Thank you, Charles, for communicating these valuable truths."

- KEN ROYER
DIRECTOR OF MISSIONARY CARE, LINK CARE CENTER

"*Revealed* is a book that challenged me as a Christian. We think that the will of God in our life is a big mystery, but Charles shows us how clearly it's laid out in the Word. Right after I got done reading this book, I literally got on my knees and asked for forgiveness! You should pick up a copy of this book and open up your mind to what you'll learn—and be ready to take action!"

- KIMANZI CONSTABLE
AUTHOR, INTERNATIONAL SPEAKER AND CONSULTANT
BLOGGER AT KIMANZICONSTABLE.COM

"In today's culture, discerning God's will can be like looking for a needle in the wrong haystack! In this book, Charles Specht clears away the clutter by providing a treasure trove of insights into the will of God. It's refreshing, biblical, and invigorating as it launches you into God's world and His will for your life. I was personally encouraged and challenged to rethink my view of God's will especially as it relates to evangelism and the Great Commission. Read, enjoy, and be ready to be challenged by it."

- RICK HOPPE
TEACHING PASTOR, FAITH BIBLE CHURCH
PROFESSOR, THE CORNERSTONE SEMINARY

"As a pastor, the most common questions I receive revolve around discovering God's will. I think most believers want to do God's will. They simply aren't sure where or how to find it. That's why I'm thankful Charles tackled this subject. I'm excited about this *Revealed* project. The church needs it!"

- RON EDMONDSON
SENIOR PASTOR, IMMANUEL BAPTIST CHURCH
BLOGGER AT RONEDMONDSON.COM

"What does God want me to do? The question most of us ask on a regular basis. *Revealed* is the answer. It challenges us to stop questioning what God wants out of our tomorrows and start doing today what God has already asked us to do. It is a refreshingly honest look at God's will and how walking in the light of His will today gives us freedom to follow Him more closely tomorrow."

- SHANNON MILHOLLAND
WRITER AND CHRISTIAN WOMEN'S EVENT SPEAKER
BLOGGER AT SHANNONMILHOLLAND.COM

"*Revealed* is written straight from a pastor's heart. It's a call for you to find your purpose and a map to living an authentic life."

- SKIP PRICHARD
FORMER CEO, INGRAM CONTENT GROUP, INC.
SPEAKER & BLOGGER AT SKIPPRICHARD.COM

"May God bless *Revealed* and use it for His glory, for the spread of His fame, and to produce a more obedient Christian who knows and understands His will."

- TRISHA RAMOS
CHRISTIAN RADIO & TELEVISION PERSONALITY
BLOGGER AT FISHWITHTRISH.COM

REVEALED

REVEALED

GOD'S WILL FOR YOUR LIFE

CHARLES **SPECHT**

Ellechor
PUBLISHING HOUSE

www.ellechorpublishinghouse.com

This book is dedicated to my beloved wife, Kathy,
and our five children, Camden, Brady, Amelia,
Charlotte, and Luke.

May God's will be done in our lives and for His
ultimate glory alone.

TABLE OF CONTENTS

TO THE READER

If you didn't already know, discovering God's will for your life was never meant to be an annoying, stressful, or even a cruel process to endure. In fact, it should really be thought of as both an exciting and spirit-lifting journey that we get to enjoy for an entire lifetime!

Determining God's plan for your life isn't the sort of journey that should feel like an endless, walk-in-a-circle trip around a desert without a compass. It's important for us to realize that God is not a god who plays games with creatures created in His own image, dangling carrots before the eyes of His beloved children. And that's the very reason why discovering God's plan for your life is God's very best plan for you.

In this book I am going to be asking and—Lord willing—answering some important questions about what it truly means to be head-over-heels in love with Jesus Christ. I want us to wade through the refreshing waters of what it actually means to be a passionate disciple of Jesus Christ, not merely a contemporary churchgoer stumbling through the motions of American Christianity. There is quite a big difference between the two, after all.

For many readers, this book will be a wonderful means of encouragement and spiritual assurance. For many others, however, all I can say is that I pray it would challenge you to evaluate your relationship with God and cause you to fall on your face, pleading for mercy on your soul. I trust that by the end of the closing chapter, God will have revealed to you which of the two you really are: a radical disciple of Jesus Christ, or a church-attending poser enjoying the convenience of a watered-down Christianity.

In case you're wondering, this is not a book about criticizing genuine believers who are struggling to know what the Lord wants them to do with their life. Nor is it something as shallow as peddling a quick 12-step approach to God's best plan for your life. No, not at all. There are plenty of books out there like that, but I'm not looking to throw fuel on that fire. My desire is to see Christians get energized about their faith and intentional about loving God and serving one another. Like most of the Christians I know, I desire to learn what the Bible teaches about adoring Christ and serving Him with real, heartfelt passion—the kind of passion that would make Christ marvel at the greatness of our faith.

With that being my objective for writing this book, I must inevitably highlight the marching orders which Christ issued for our local churches today. Frankly, it's not a topic many American Christians are comfortable talking about, but that's precisely why it's so critical that we do. Ultimately, it's the very foundation to discerning God's will in your own life today.

CHAPTER ONE

GOD'S WILL: RADICAL LOVE

"For God has not given us a spirit of timidity, but of power and love and discipline." (2 Timothy 1:7)

"God delights in using ordinary Christians who come to the end of themselves and choose to trust in his extraordinary provision. He stands ready to allocate his power to all who are radically dependent on him and radically devoted to making much of him." —David Platt

AN OCEAN LINER was slicing across the Pacific when its captain spotted an S-O-S smoke signal ascending from what was thought to be a small and deserted island. As the rescuers landed ashore, an old man standing in front of three man-made structures greeted them joyfully. The man had been stranded alone on the island for nearly twenty-five years.

Wondering about the three huts along the tree line, the captain asked him, "Is there anyone else on this island?"

1

"Just me," came the reply.

"Then why do you have three buildings?"

"Well, y'see," said the skinny old man, "the one on the left is my house, and the one in the middle is my church."

"What about the one on the right?" the captain asked.

"Oh, that's my *old* church. I stopped going there years ago. Too many hypocrites, y'see."

Christians tend to laugh at comical stories like this one, but there also happens to be a real sense in which much of our modern-day American Christianity is a lot like that lonely, shipwrecked old man. Far too often, Christians church-shop and church-hop with hardly a second thought about whether or not it's actually in their best interest to do so. If the pastor leaves, the style of music changes, or the deacons paint a new color on the walls, we can always find another church. Maybe even a *better* one, we surmise. We assume the grass is always greener on the other side of the holy hill, and many times it most certainly is. Indeed, the grass may be greener at some of the other churches around your city, but what we often fail to appreciate is that someone still has to mow it!

There are *issues* in just about every church around the world.

CHURCHES ARE LIKE A BOX OF CHOCOLATES

Personally, I have literally been to dozens of churches during my lifetime. Without exception, each one had meticulously crafted their own special blend of what "church" ought to look like. From a bird's-eye view, many of them appeared

2

to be quite healthy, flourishing with an abundance of God-exalting, Christ-loving disciples. Some of the other churches, however, might be better off doing nothing more than showing up next Sunday and voting for a do-over.

Maybe you've visited a few churches like that as well?

I've visited mega-churches with thousands of members, new church-plants where having thirty people show up was something to rejoice about, and churches that met behind steel doors in a cold prison facility. I've been to churches with audio sound systems that cost more than a Rolls Royce, and to churches that met in school classrooms with no microphones at all. I visited one church where the lone usher was a college student wearing a Superman t-shirt, and others where every usher had gray hair and wore a pressed suit and tie.

There are churches with soft padded pews and churches with hard metal chairs; churches with ornately-carved wooden pulpits and churches with only music stands; home churches that meet in someone's living room and churches with multiple super-sanctuaries; churches with a warm, inviting atmosphere and churches that are so unfriendly even Mr. Iscariot would have blushed. Some churches permit only hymns to be sung while others wouldn't know what a hymnal was if you shoved one under their nose.

The fact of the matter is that there are tens of thousands of churches to choose from, and they're each filled with fascinating people from all walks of life. One thing I have noticed, however, is that there is no such thing as the *perfect* church. Someone once jokingly said me, "Charles, if you ever find the perfect church, do them a favor and don't ever go there. You'd just mess it up for everyone else."

So that begs an important question: Which church is actually doing "church" right?

THE KIND OF CHURCH JESUS WOULD ATTEND

Chapters two and three in the book of Revelation provide us with seven letters authored by Jesus Himself—penned at the hand of the apostle John—and delivered to seven real churches in seven different cities. Those seven churches, essentially, are representative of all Christian churches everywhere in the world today. What strikes me as odd, however, is that Jesus told five of those churches to flat-out repent of their wickedness, or something awful was going to happen. And soon. He even threatened to permanently shut the doors of one church forever.

Five out of seven churches. That's not very good.

Of the two churches that Jesus had only kind words to say about, one was a church enduring severe tribulation, poverty, and religious persecution.[1] The other church was one that Jesus said kept His word, did not deny His name, and kept the word of His perseverance.[2] In other words, Jesus commended only those churches filled with people wholly devoted to glorifying Him, regardless of what it cost them in the end. What impressed the glorified Son of God was not how popular or well attended a church had become, but how obsessed the saints were about declaring His holy name before a sin-loving world.

---

1 The church in Smyrna; see Revelation 2:8-11
2 The church in Philadelphia; see Revelation 3:7-13

If you had asked Jesus to recommend a good church in the area, it's unlikely He would have sent you down the street to that state-of-the-art, multi-million dollar church facility. Nor maybe even to the one on the other side of town with the hip worship band and trendy youth program. No, He probably would have told you to pack your bags and move to Smyrna, because that was where His people were enduring intense persecution, remaining faithful to His word, and persevering in their faith—even if it killed them in the end.

What I find so intriguing is that the Lord's commendations had absolutely nothing to do with the church's stylistic approach to music, the sort of facility they fellowshipped in, which translation of the Bible they read from, the size of their membership, or even the multi-faceted demographics of the worshippers who showed up Sunday morning. Nor was Christ concerned about whether or not the pastor wore a suit and tie when he preached or mere faded blue jeans and sneakers. What concerned Jesus was how radical the people were about loving Him, not how loyal they were to a particular preacher, church denomination, or even the showy frills of a seeker-sensitive religion.

Ultimately, Jesus was satisfied only with those churches committed to pursuing God-centered worship, not shallow veneration. Radical love was the decisive issue as far as Jesus was concerned, not vain popularity.

I think there is a lot to be learned by understanding that.

Question: If Jesus were to write a letter to your church today, what do you think He would say? Would He applaud the faithfulness of your local congregation, encouraging the attendees to forge ahead with business as usual? Do you think Jesus would have anything to say to you personally? Yes, to you personally. Do you think He would demand that some of the churchgoers in your congregation repent of their sin, wickedness, and lack of commitment? Do you think He would threaten to forever close the doors of your local church assembly?

Five out of seven churches. Again, that's not very good.

GOD-CENTERED WORSHIP IS GOD'S WILL FOR YOU

In his book *Today's Evangelism*, Ernest C. Reisinger wrote, "The church that does not evangelize will fossilize, that is, dry up and become useless to Christ and the world."[3] Without question, God doesn't desire for you or the people in your local church to fossilize, dry up, or become useless to Christ and the world. In fact, He wants just the opposite. God wants every one of you crazy in love with Him.

Christians who are laser-focused on God's will for their life are passionate about God and thoroughly engaged in the battle over the souls of men, women, and children, whether they be saved or unsaved. As God's adopted children, we're to be constantly involved in the process of discipling any and all who profess genuine claims of saving faith. I prefer to think of this spiritual war for both the salvation and progressive sanctification of genuine believers as "Great Commission Discipleship."

The Great Commission mandate Christ gave to the Church centers on the exciting ministry of "teaching

3 Ernest C. Reisinger, <u>Today's Evangelism</u> (Craig Press, 1982), page XV.

them to observe all that I commanded you."[4] The Great Commission, then, has as much to do with developing your own Christ-likeness as it does with you actually getting saved in the first place. God is not merely concerned about the reality of your spiritual conversion. He is immensely passionate about your progressive discipleship as well.

Author and pastor John MacArthur put it this way, "The kind of evangelism called for in this commission does not end with the conversion of the unbeliever."[5] Another way to say it is that Jesus is interested in your radical discipleship, not so much about how many people show up at your church service next Sunday morning.

Yet we cannot overlook the fact that a significant aspect of our personal discipleship finds its very roots in our obedience to share the gospel with those around us—both locally and around the world. It is for this very reason that God is keeping you alive right now.

MacArthur also wrote, "There is only one reason the Lord allows His church to remain on earth: to seek and to save the lost, just as Christ's only reason for coming to earth was to seek and to save the lost....Therefore, a believer who is not committed to winning the lost for Jesus Christ should reexamine his relationship to the Lord and certainly his divine reason for existence."[6]

Are you that kind of radically engaged believer? Would Jesus marvel at the greatness of your faith? Do you love the people at your church with a relentless, consuming love?

---

4 Matthew 28:20
5 John MacArthur, The MacArthur Study Bible (Thomas Nelson, Inc, 2006), note on Matthew 28:20; page 1419.
6 John MacArthur, The MacArthur New Testament Commentary, Matthew 24-28 (The Moody Bible Institute of Chicago, 1989), page 333.

Can you say, like the apostle Paul did to the Philippian believers, "For God is my witness, how I long for you all with the affection of Christ Jesus," and not feel like a liar if you did?[7] Do you desire to know God and serve Him more passionately? Are you at war against the lusts of this world, battling for the souls of those around you? How concerned are you about your own spiritual development? Are you actively and deliberately involved in the Lord's plan for your life today?

Let's find out.

---

7 Philippians 1:8

CHAPTER TWO

GOD'S WILL: FRUITFUL MINISTRY

"If you abide in Me, and My words abide in you, ask whatever you wish, and it will be done for you. My Father is glorified by this, that you bear much fruit, and so prove to be My disciples. Just as the Father has loved Me, I have loved you; abide in My love." (John 15:7-9)

"None of us consistently produces actions that verify our faith in Christ. We drift in and out of godly living. Yet our hope is not in how well we live but in how well Christ lived—and died—on our behalf." —Charles Swindoll

HAVE YOU EVER wondered what God wants you to do with your life? Maybe you think about it all the time. Ever wondered what ministry He wants you to get involved with? Exactly what does God expect from His beloved children anyway?

When Life Throws You a Curve Ball

I was a senior in college the day God lifted the veil from my eyes, saving my sin-sick soul. Although I was so very grateful to be saved, I also knew that God had thrown a holy wrench into my life's plan. At the time, I was a psychology student in the last year of my undergraduate studies. I had planned to immediately enroll into a master's degree program and eventually into a doctoral program for clinical psychology. My life's ambition up to that point was to eventually hang a few diplomas on an office wall, purchase a black leather couch, and have my disturbed patients pay me $250 an hour while I interpreted their dreams. Psychologist Charles. That was the plan.

After a few weeks of being saved, however, I developed a problem. I had lost all interest in being a psychologist and now wanted only to learn more about my precious Savior. The problem for me was that I really had no clue how to actually do that. I wasn't a member of a local church, and I didn't even understand why I should become one. Nor did I have a clue about what criteria a Christian should use when picking a church to attend. Being only a babe in Christ, I didn't even know what made a theologically conservative church different from a liberal, anything-goes church. I knew only a handful of people who claimed to know Christ, and I really had no idea what to do next.

I remember kneeling in my dorm room, praying, *Lord, why didn't You just zap me into Heaven? Why am I still here? What do You want me to do with my life? I just spent four years of my life preparing to be something I no longer want to be. What do You want from me, God? I'll do anything; just show me what You want me to do.*

That was essentially my prayer. And if I've learned anything since those first few weeks of walking with God, it is that Christians all around the world are also asking their Maker the very same questions.

Have you ever asked God questions like these? Maybe you are asking Him those questions right now. Thankfully, God has already given you the answer in His Bible.

THE CAT IS OUT OF THE BAG

God's answer to those questions is essentially this: *As long as you are glorifying Me while making both yourself and others into genuine disciples of Jesus Christ, go ahead and do whatever you want!* That is precisely God's will for your life today. You're to find your singular satisfaction in God while conforming others into the image of Jesus Christ. It really is a rather simple and yet marvelously refreshing assignment. Love God with everything you are and then do whatever your heart desires. What a plan!

This disciple-making mission is the Church's core ministry today, tomorrow, and up until Jesus returns to take us home. God's desire for every Christian is that we passionately worship Him while selflessly serving others. Great Commission Discipleship is the sole reason God gave each of His children supernatural spiritual gifts. It's also why He provided the local church with gifted men to equip us for this crucial task. As a saved and sanctified Christ-loving disciple, you are sufficiently and miraculously armed for the ministry of Great Commission Discipleship.

The local church's mission of glorifying God while making Christ-like disciples of all the nations is to be the priority of our earthly existence. It is the very reason you are here on Earth and not in Heaven right now. There are literally tens of thousands of ministries in which you could make Christ-like disciples, but every activity must be tested in the fires of holy living and—particularly—keeping your eyes fixed on the trophy of God's magnanimous glory. Maintaining such a radical ambition is not always easy (it rarely is), but it certainly is God's will for you today.

ANY TIME FOR JESUS?

Recently I was talking to a man who lives in my neighborhood. It was a gorgeous Sunday afternoon, and he asked what I had planned for later that day. I told him that my family usually attends church on Sunday evenings. Flabbergasted, he questioned how many hours I spent at church every Sunday. After tallying up the two morning services and an evening service, I confessed, "We probably go to church for about six hours every Sunday." I'll never forget his response. With a look of absolute horror, he said, "That's a lot of God!"

And that's precisely the problem with the world today. Most people don't mind the *idea* of God; they just prefer not having a lot of *God* on the agenda.

Horatius Bonar, a respected Scottish pastor from the nineteenth century, summarized the goal of Christianity when he wrote, "Our position is such that we cannot remain neutral. Our life cannot be one of harmless obscurity. We must either repel or attract—save or ruin souls!"[8]

When it comes down to it, that's God's will for your life today. He wants you to not remain neutral and to passionately save or ruin souls. Frankly, if Christianity is worth anything at all to you, it must be worth absolutely everything to you.

GOD'S LOVE FOR THE UNLOVABLE

The first sermon I ever preached in my life was back in 1998. I was locked up in jail at the time, surrounded by thieves, drug dealers, and murderers. It was a very good day.

I was ministering at one of California's many jail facilities, and it was my first time ever serving as a religious volunteer. I've never been more nervous in my life. And yet, I have rarely experienced more joy in ministry than when I've been locked behind barred doors preaching the gospel to captured citizens awaiting their final verdict.

It was during that very first year of ministering in a county jail that I met an inmate whom I prefer to call Michael.

Michael was a young, energetic black kid who had lived a thoroughly wretched lifestyle of rampant crime and drug abuse. He was born and raised in a culture not unlike most living inside the slammer: rough neighborhood, crime, prostitution, unbridled pressures from neighborhood gangs. He was just another nameless face in a long laundry list of criminal statistics. What set Michael apart from the other inmates, however, was that he had attempted to murder his own father while under the influence of drugs. During his first few days

8 Horatius Bonar, <u>Words to Winners of Souls</u> (Presbyterian and Reformed Publishing Company, 1995), page 14.

in jail, sobriety settled in, and Michael was forced to deal with the permanent, life-altering consequences of his sin.

It was not a very good week for him.

Soon thereafter, Michael began attending my chapel services, which at that time were held a few days every week. Of the hundred or so inmates who would attend each service, Michael was one of the few souls who lingered afterward to talk, asking important questions like, "What happens after you die?" and "Can God ever forgive me?"

The Holy Spirit convicted Michael's heart over those weeks, and, since I was available at that time, the Lord chose to use me as His instrument for discipleship. A short while later, Michael placed his trust in Christ and made an open profession of faith in Jesus as his personal Lord and Savior.

THE ROAD TO CHRISTIAN SANCTIFICATION

One of the incredible features of our American penal system is that all manner of religious literature (the good, the bad, and the utterly blasphemous) is readily available to the inmates, and usually upon demand. An inmate can even get their hands on a satanic bible if they put in a formal request. I would often find myself preaching to men who had attended—just an hour or two before—a New Age, Muslim, Hindu, Buddhist, or some other "religious" worship service. It seemed as though the enemy had no shortage of laborers for its cause. Jail can easily become a tangled smorgasbord of religion for an undiscerning soul searching for answers to the meaning of life.

As the weeks flew by, I learned that Michael had been reading certain religious literature that, frankly, peddled some rather poor theology. After a particular chapel service one afternoon, I told Michael that I would buy him a quality Bible that contained many study notes, and that he should throw away everything else he was filtering into his mind. He happily agreed. Within a week I was able to personally hand-deliver that Bible to him. Michael began feasting on the Word regularly for hours at a time and throughout his day (inmates have a lot of spare time on their hands). I remember having many blessed conversations with him and was thankful to the Lord for the work being done in Michael's heart.

RIGHTING THE WRONGS OF THE PAST

A few months later, Michael mustered up some courage and asked me to help him repair the shattered relationship he had with his father. I was skeptical at first and unsure how I could possibly be of any help, but I agreed nevertheless. It turned out that my role would be little more than helping facilitate telephone conversations between a father and his estranged son.

From the noisy confines of his overcrowded cellblock, Michael called me collect on the telephone, and I then dialed his father for a three-way conversation. From the first moment I spoke to Michael's father, it was apparent he wanted nothing more in this world than to restore the severed relationship with his son. His dad kept calling me "sir" (I was only in my early twenties at the time), and after saying a few things to get the conversation rolling, my job was to sit back and do nothing more than listen.

It seemed odd—eavesdropping on those heartwarming

and personal conversations—but I could hear the pleasure in Michael's father's voice whenever his son confessed his sins, begging for forgiveness. I remember sitting on my couch, feeling quite uncomfortable, yet listening intently to that father and son ask one another for a second chance. It was so very precious.

A number of weeks passed by, along with another telephone call or two, and Michael wrote me letters often, thanking me for everything I was doing in his life. I must confess that I didn't feel as though I was really going out of my way to do much for him, but whatever God was doing through me was precisely what Michael needed at the time. And he was so very grateful for it.

The final verdict was eventually rendered in Michael's court case. He was subsequently sentenced to several more years behind bars, this time in a penitentiary. When he no longer showed up for my chapel services, I knew he'd been transferred to the state penitentiary, and that meant the end of our relationship. At least in this life.

The discipleship ministry I had with Michael was not altogether unique when compared to other relationships two people might have with each other. With Michael, I would usually do the teaching and he'd be the one listening to God's Word, trying to obey it. On more than a few occasions, however, I'm quite certain I learned a lot more from Michael than he ever gleaned from me.

WHAT ARE YOU DEVOTED TO?

One of the most powerful verses having to do with understanding God's will for your life has got to be Acts 2:42, which says of those early believers, "They were continually devoting themselves to the apostles' teaching and to fellowship, to the breaking of bread and to prayer." In just this one verse we learn what is essentially the uncompromising lifestyle of a radical disciple of Jesus Christ.

True disciples of Christianity are people who regularly devote themselves to the apostles' teaching (the Bible), to fellowship with other like-minded believers, to the celebration of communion in the breaking of bread, and to prayer. But don't overlook what else that verse says. The Holy Spirit makes a point to tell us those early believers were *continually devoting themselves* to these activities.

Question: Did you catch that? Don't miss this point. Understanding (and heeding) this concept is the bedrock foundation for determining God's will in your life. The Lord is unlikely to further reveal His plan for the direction of your life if you are not first devoting yourself to the things He's already disclosed.

Please notice that no one had to motivate those early disciples toward holiness, worship, or active participation in ministry. They passionately loved the Lord their God with all their heart, mind, soul, and strength. Church mailings, reminder notices discreetly tucked inside the Sunday church bulletin, and weekly emails from the pastor were all equally unnecessary. Radical obedience to Jesus Christ was nonoptional behavior as far as they were each concerned. They were *devoting themselves* to these spiritual disciplines, and were continuously doing so.

More Than Just a Church Service

Those early Christians were deliberate about their walk with God, passionate about their communion with Christ, and intentional about their love for one another. They walked the Christian walk and talked the holy talk. They lived a lifestyle of sanctified boldness sprinkled with consecrated speech. The early church's discipleship program was one of thorough regularity and affectionate devotion to their God and one another. They spent hours in each other's homes throughout the week and regularly conversed about the glorious God of their common salvation.

They didn't allow their Christianity to be defined by a seventy-five-minute Sunday morning worship service, with an occasional midweek Bible study inserted here and there. No, not hardly. Their focus was on the glory of their God seven days a week. *"Day by day* continuing with one mind in the temple, and breaking bread from house to house, they were taking their meals together with gladness and sincerity of heart, praising God and having favor with all the people"* (emphasis mine).[9]

Their day-by-day fervor resulted in God moving among them in constant, miraculous ways. Notice the fruit of their passionate zeal for Christ-centered ministry there in the city of Jerusalem: "And the Lord was adding to their number *day by day* those who were being saved" (emphasis mine).[10]

Did you catch that? Day-by-day discipleship resulted in the daily winning of souls. No doubt God is trying to tell us something important here about living for His glory

---

9 Acts 2:46
10 Acts 2:47

every single day of our lives. This is the key to unlocking God's revealed will for your life today. When your attention is focused squarely on the God of your salvation, the blurry things in life tend to become crystal clear.

DON'T PRACTICE WHAT GOD HATES

Do you ever wonder sometimes if today's American Church just doesn't get it? Does it seem like we are missing something important? What about you personally? Are you continually devoting yourself to the resolute worship of the Triune God, or has something else been hoarding your time and attention? What have you been giving yourself over to lately? If you are not passionate about worshipping the God of the Bible, then to what idol have you been burning incense lately?

The spectrum of Great Commission Discipleship is vast and wide, spanning from when you first heard the gospel, to the moment God regenerated your soul, and up until you exhale your final breath. In other words, the progressive sanctification process of passionate, Christ-centered discipleship will last your entire lifetime. It is God's will for your life today.

On that discipleship spectrum, we find regenerate believers at various levels of spiritual maturity and fruitfulness. Few Christians are as uncompromising as the apostle Paul was. Yet even that mighty soldier of Christ had to battle against his own sinful rebellion now and then, for he confessed, "For what I am doing, I do not understand; for I am not practicing what I would like to do, but I am doing the very thing I hate."[11]

Do you ever find yourself practicing the very thing you hate? Why do we do that? One of the most futile things a Christian can ever do is try to discover God's *un*revealed will in their life while at the same time actively practicing the things God hates.

THE GOD OF SECOND CHANCES

Just about every believer I know has endured more than a few dry seasons of spiritual apathy. No doubt about it. In fact, most of us can probably relate quite well to the waywardness of a young man named Mark, a guy who flat-out abandoned both the apostle Paul and Barnabas when the ministry got a bit rough.[12] Yet thanks be to the Lord that genuine disciples always persevere in their faith. God never lets His children stray too far off the path of holiness. By God's grace, Mark eventually repented of his cowardice and began serving the Lord with an intentional passion. Upon learning about his subsequent change in both attitude and behavior, years later the apostle Paul instructed Timothy, saying, "Pick up Mark and bring him with you, for he is useful to me for service."[13]

Notice that it was only after Mark got serious about his faith that the apostle felt Mark had become useful to him in ministry. Paul was not at all interested in ministering alongside vacillating, uncommitted people. It was all or nothing as far as he was concerned.

---

11 Romans 7:15
12 Acts 15:36–39
13 2 Timothy 4:11

It should be all or nothing for each of us today as well.

YOU ARE A MIRACULOUS FRUIT-BEARER

You are immensely useful to God because every genuine disciple of Jesus Christ is useful to his or her heavenly Father. You are yielding an abundant and fruitful crop, "some a hundredfold, some sixty, and some thirty."[14] We're told that in biblical times, an average ratio for harvested grain to what was sown was eight to one, with a ten to one ratio considered exceptional.[15] Therefore, when Jesus preached that even the *less* fruitful Christians would still yield a thirtyfold crop, it simply blew their minds.

Active love for God always results in far more spiritual fruit than you would have ever thought possible. Pursuing God-centered worship through Christ-centered activity is precisely God's will for your life today. It's how you generate your spiritual crop.

Regardless of your own personal level of spiritual maturity, you are a prosperous, fruit-bearing disciple. No doubt about it. A tree, Jesus said, "is known by its fruit," and genuine disciples of Jesus Christ are producing a bumper harvest for the glory of God alone.[16]

Jesus said, "Let your light shine before men in such a way that they may see your good works, and glorify your Father in heaven."[17] Your life is meant to be a public display of Christ-centered worship so that God's name would be glorified before all men.

---

14 Matthew 13:8
15 John MacArthur, The MacArthur Study Bible (Thomas Nelson, Inc, 2006), note on Mark 4:8; page 1465.
16 Matthew 12:33
17 Matthew 5:16

The apostle Paul wrote, "We are His workmanship, created in Christ Jesus for good works, which God prepared beforehand so that we would walk in them."[18] You are God's regenerated pottery, sculpted for affectionate submission and consecrated living.

Regarding the expected lifestyle for all people attending church, Paul told Timothy, "Instruct them to do good, to be rich in good works, to be generous and ready to share, storing up for themselves the treasure of a good foundation for the future, so that they may take hold of that which is life indeed."[19] The men, women, and children of biblical Christianity deny worldly pleasure, consider the needs of others as more important than their own, and flourish in Great Commission living. That is God's will for all of His adopted children. It is His desire for you as well.

At the end of the day, nominal churchgoers produce only a dead and fruitless faith, but genuine Christians blow the roof off Heaven's silo!

CHRIST-CENTERED LIVING IS
LIKE BUILDING A HOUSE

There was a rundown, ramshackle-of-a-house in my neighborhood that was an eyesore to everyone who drove by it. Including me. I was thrilled when a local contractor purchased it a few years back. He had planned to fix it up and then flip it for a tidy profit. His workers soon tore down most of the old shell and began framing new walls for the structure. Their work looked very promising. However, when the economy took a nosedive shortly thereafter, the

18 Ephesians 2:10
19 1 Timothy 6:18-19

homebuilder ran out of money, and the half-built house remained half-built for another two years. It was even more of an eyesore at that time, if you can believe it.

Thankfully, it didn't stay half-built forever.

Someone eventually erected a fence around the entire property and set up a large display containing an architect's drawing of what the future home would someday look like. It was a beautiful rendering of the final product. A few weeks later, new workers arrived and began finishing what the laborers from two years ago had left undone. Today, the home looks to be about 90% complete. The entire neighborhood is looking forward to the day it finally gets finished, once and for all.

Have you ever noticed that there are a lot of American churchgoers sort of like that old rundown house? Spiritually speaking, they are half-built disciples. An unfinished, incomplete work. They lack a sustaining joy, and, frankly, many are practically an eyesore to behold. Yet when a faithful believer comes alongside them—investing their time, love, and attention into that person's life—the eventual result will be a beautiful rendering of Christ-likeness.

WHEN GOD BUILDS A HOUSE

Have you ever driven by a jobsite where construction workers were building a house? The process of Great Commission Discipleship is somewhat similar to that. The workers carefully pour and level the foundation, but only after laboring to prepare the soil by digging deep trenches. Once the foundation has been laid and leveled, other workers then frame the walls and install other features of the structure according to the designer's master plan.

Such work is similar to the radical ministry of building the dwelling place of God—the Body of Christ. The apostle Paul wrote that genuine believers have been "built on the foundation of the apostles and prophets, Christ Jesus Himself being the cornerstone, in whom the whole building, being fitted together, is growing into a holy temple in the Lord, in whom you also are being built together into a dwelling of God in the Spirit."[20]

Now that is radical love!

Did you know that true disciples of Jesus Christ are like holy bricks which our heavenly Father fits together? If you're a true believer, then you're one of God's bricks. Every one of us is molded, sculpted, and permanently set into the mortar of His unfailing love. As each soul turns from his or her sin, getting saved by His omnipotent grace, the edifice grows into something God calls *holy*. Together, with each individual brick, the divine Mason places us side by side—as He sees fit—and calls us His dwelling place.

His house. His home. His Temple. His Bride. His Church. His family.

I don't know about you, but I think that's outstanding!

---

20 Ephesians 2:20-22

CHAPTER THREE

GOD'S WILL:
CLEARLY DEFINED

"For this is the will of God, your sanctification; that is, that you abstain from sexual immorality." (1 Thessalonians 4:3)

"It is impossible to do everything people want you to do. You have just enough time to do God's will. If you can't get it all done, it means you're trying to do more than God intended for you to do (or, possibly, that you're watching too much television)." —Rick Warren

I N CASE YOU haven't noticed, road signs are rather helpful bits of metal and paint. They're practically everywhere. You will find them in private alleys, on most street corners in residential neighborhoods, hanging on the walls in teenagers' bedrooms, in bumper-to-bumper highway traffic, and along old country roads where there's not a soul in sight for hundreds of miles. Essentially, road signs are designed to accomplish three main things: direct driving behavior, provide information, and keep people safe.

There are road signs that announce which city is up ahead, the legal speed limit a person may drive, the height clearance of bridges and overpasses, and even where the nearest hotels and restaurants can be found. In fact, if it weren't for street signs, we'd all get lost a lot more, have more accidents, not know whether to stop or go, and we'd have a terrible time finding the nearest Chinese restaurant (which would certainly be the worst of all).

WHEN GOD GIVES YOU A SIGN

Wouldn't it be amazing if knowing God's will for your life was as simple as obeying traffic signs? Wouldn't it be helpful if you were traveling down one of life's roads and a sign from God suddenly appeared right before you, saying, "The college you should attend is at the next exit. Turn right ahead"? Or maybe, "The job you have been praying for is coming up on your left fast. Merge now and follow the arrows." Or even, "The man you've been praying about marrying is dark, handsome, and not the guy you're having dinner with right now. Keep moving."

Yes, I suppose most people would simply love a few signs from God like that. I know that I would. But the funny thing is that God has actually been giving you those signs ever since you were born. No, seriously, it's the truth. God has told you many times what His will is for your life. In fact, you've probably read and been told what God's will is countless times before, but simply didn't recognize it for what it was.

What do I mean by that? What I mean is that God has already written down His plan for your life and given it to you free of charge. You see, phrases like "God's will," "the Lord's will," and "will of God" appear in the Bible numerous times. These phrases are the specifics regarding God's plan for you. God provided you with signs. He has told each of us what to do and what not to do, time and time again.

The problem with many of us, however, is that rather than obeying what God has already revealed, we opt for rebellion, deciding instead to wait for another sign more to our liking or pointing toward a more *desirable* destination.

DON'T IGNORE THE SIGNS GOD GIVES

For example, rather than remaining sexually pure until marriage, some people choose to indulge in unrestrained fornication and/or internet pornography, and then wonder why God won't give them another sign, even when they pray for one as often as they do. They reject God's revealed opportunities for obedience left and right, yet have the gall to actually accuse God of withholding the *good* things from them.

You've never done that, have you?

Rather than being obedient to God by ministering to the needs of others around them, some people remain defiant to the mandate of counting others as more important than themselves and, instead, live a life of wanton lust, pleasure-seeking, and a boastful pride of life. When the twists, turns, and valleys of life don't lead them to the destination they were hoping for, they wonder where in the world God is and why He isn't doing more for them.

Yes, I do believe this is a blunder that even Christians sometimes commit.

God has provided signs for your life. He has fully disclosed what you should and shouldn't do. The issue is whether you'll obey the omniscient Planner or just keep right on driving down the highway of life, saying, "Yeah, I know that was the exit God wanted me to take, but I'm hoping for another one a bit more to my liking, thank you very much!" Or, "Yes, I know that sign said no sexual fornication up ahead, but I'm just going to keep traveling in that direction anyway, cross my fingers, and hope I don't drive off the cliff."

Again, have you ever done that? Are you doing that right now? If you are, then stop! There is absolutely no reason to assume God would ever disclose His *un*revealed will for your life until you're first obedient in what He has *already* revealed.

God Always Prevails in the End

This do-what-feels-right-in-the-moment mentality reminds me of a guy in the Old Testament named Jonah. Jonah happened to be one of God's specially anointed prophets. God told him to go to Nineveh and preach the gospel. Jonah thought, "Nope!" and immediately boarded a ship sailing in the opposite direction.

God was not amused.

A vicious storm appeared out of nowhere, and the ship's crew eventually tossed Jonah into the sea. Rather than drowning, he was subsequently swallowed whole by a large fish. He nestled in the acidic belly of that fish for three long days and three long nights. Apparently Jonah had a bitter aftertaste, because the fish vomited him onto the beach. The disgraced prophet then stood up, combed the bile out of his hair, brushed the sand off his tunic, and marched all the way to Nineveh to preach.

It's amazing how God always gets His way in the end. The Lord's plan always comes to fruition. No man or woman ever frustrates the omnipotent King. And that's why I believe this chapter should prove most helpful to you. That is, unless you want to have your own little Jonah experience?

What we're going to do now is look at several passages of Scripture that specifically use the phrase "God's will," "will of the Lord," or "will of God." By doing this you'll be able to more accurately discern God's desire for your life, both today and tomorrow. What you are about to read is God's actual revealed plan for your life *today*!

GOD'S WILL IS THAT YOU BE SAVED

God the Father sent His only begotten Son into this world to die on a cross—for you! He didn't do it for any reason other than that you might be saved. It is not God's desire that people remain defiant, wicked, prideful, or eternally Hell-bound. God wants to save people—a people for His own pleasure. It is His awesome plan. It's how God the Father builds a family for Himself. He absolutely loves adoption, and all those who trust God become the adopted siblings of Jesus Christ. God has one *biological* Son, yet He is currently gathering millions and millions of adopted children. Jesus said, "For whoever does the *will of God*, he is my brother and sister and mother" (emphasis mine).[21]

One of the ways God draws people to Himself in order to save them is by allowing them to be sorrowful to the point of repentance. Paul wrote to the Corinthians, saying, "I now rejoice, not that you were made sorrowful, but that you were made sorrowful to the point of repentance; for you were made sorrowful according to the *will of God*, so that you might not suffer loss in anything through us. For the sorrow that is according to the *will of God* produces a repentance without regret, leading to salvation, but the sorrow of the world produces death" (emphasis mine).[22] When a person is broken over his or her own sin, God uses it to draw that person to Himself. This plan in the will of God does not lead to sorrow for God's child, but to everlasting peace.

Once you place your faith in Jesus Christ alone, you receive an enduring desire for the things of God that lasts for all eternity. The apostle John wrote, "The world is passing away, and also its lust; but the one who does the *will of God* lives forever" (emphasis mine).[23] To be singularly focused on God's glory and His plan for your life is precisely the reason God saved you in the first place. It is His will.

GOD'S WILL IS THAT YOU BE PROGRESSIVELY SANCTIFIED

On the heels of salvation comes the wonderful work of progressive sanctification. Sanctification is the process of

---

21 Mark 3:35
22 2 Corinthians 7:9-10
23 1 John 2:17

spiritual maturity. It is the life-long process of being molded into the image of Jesus Christ—of sinning less and becoming godlier—each and every day. This process of sanctification takes on many forms and manifests itself in every facet of a Christian's life, including your thoughts, words, actions, decisions, and behaviors. One place this process of sanctification becomes noticeably evident is in the realm of sexual purity.

Paul wrote to the believers in Thessalonica, "For this is the *will of God*, your sanctification; that is, that you abstain from sexual immorality" (emphasis mine).[24] Adultery, fornication, premarital sex, pornography, and every other form of sexual misconduct is wrong, sinful, and directly in opposition to the will of God. If you're committing sexual transgression—whether in secret or public, in any form whatsoever—then you are not performing God's revealed will for your life. There's absolutely no reason to think God would ever disclose new information to you about His plan until you first repent of your sexual sin, refocusing your mind on Christ-centered sanctification.

This is a serious and most necessary requirement for all of God's children. It is amazing how often we tend to pray for the knowledge of God's plan in various areas of our lives, yet hide known sin behind our backs with a veiled hand. The writer to the Hebrews wrote, "For you have need of endurance, so that when you have done the *will of God*, you may receive what was promised" (emphasis mine).[25] The will of God is revealed to those who endure, persevere, and triumph over temptation, particularly in the area of sexual activity.

---

24 1 Thessalonians 4:3
25 Hebrews 10:36

When we forsake God's plan of sanctification—in exchange for the passing pleasures of sin for a moment—we forfeit tremendous blessings from our Father. The apostle Peter wrote that Christians should conduct themselves "so as to live the rest of the time in the flesh no longer for the lusts of men, but for the *will of God*" (emphasis mine).[26] God's revealed plan for your life is based on sexual purity.

A second major area in which Christians are to be sanctified is in the area of substance abuse or intake. Believers are not to be finding their kicks and enjoyments from the abuse of things like drugs and alcohol, for example. Those vices lead to the world's bedroom, not God's throne room. Many people—even many contemporary American Christians—consider such advice as outdated and rather prudish. But God doesn't. In fact, God warns His children to "not be foolish, but understand what the *will of the Lord* is. And do not get drunk with wine, for that is dissipation, but be filled with the Spirit" (emphasis mine).[27] There is certainly a considerable difference between enjoying a single glass of fine wine and being wasted drunk at a sorority party, but each person must choose for him- or herself how to live wisely in this critical area of life. God says His will is not drunkenness, but Spirit-filled living.

How are you doing in these two areas of your progressive sanctification? Please understand that if you've been indulging in internet pornography, sexual fornication, or drunkenness, it's unlikely that God will give you more information about what to do in life. Sexual purity and Spirit-filled sobriety are

---

26 1 Peter 4:2
27 Ephesians 5:17–18

important on God's list for discerning His will. We should consider them utterly important as well.

GOD'S WILL IS FOR YOU TO BE THANKFUL

Another aspect of God's will for your life is that you be a thankful person. It would seem natural for someone who is saved, having the Holy Spirit abiding in them 24/7, to be a thankful person. But far too often we are nothing of the sort. How bizarre. Strange, really. Being thankful is the mark of a genuine child of God, and God's will for you is to be a person who demonstrates uncompromising thankfulness.

Every one of God's children is at a different state of spiritual maturity and sanctification, but thankfulness would seem to be an area of life which all believers should be overwhelming conquerors in. God wants you to be thankful in every area of your life, during every circumstance of it, even when the details are not going as you had hoped.

Paul wrote to the Christians in Thessalonica, "In everything give thanks; for this is *God's will* for you in Christ Jesus" (emphasis mine).[28] It doesn't matter if the situation we find ourselves in right now is inconvenient or even uncomfortable. We are to be thankful. To not be thankful is to forfeit God's will in your life.

GOD'S WILL IS THAT YOU BE PRAYERFUL

As mentioned above, being thankful should seem almost second nature for a true believer, but there is another area

---

28 1 Thessalonians 5:18

that would seem even more natural, and that is the spiritual discipline of prayer.

Prayer is communication with God. Christians pray to God the Father, in the name of God the Son, and through the power of God's Holy Spirit. When praying, you demonstrate humility and a trust in God for what you can't do for yourself. There are many components of biblical prayer, a few of which are praise, asking God for your daily needs, petitioning God to keep you out of harm's way and from the evil one, and intercession on behalf of others. God hears your prayers and answers them, both according to His plan and for your ultimate good.

It is peculiar, then, that someone saved, sanctified, and empowered by God's Holy Spirit could pray so haphazardly.

Jesus often prayed and usually for hours at a time. The apostle Paul prayed regularly as well. While writing to the Christians in Rome, he commented that, "always in my prayers making request, if perhaps now at last by the *will of God* I may succeed in coming to you" (emphasis mine).[29] Paul knew that even his travel plans rested in the hands of God. Later in that same letter, Paul wrote, "so that I may come to you in joy by the *will of God* and find refreshing rest in your company" (emphasis mine).[30]

When praying to God, we speak, listen, and react. We're telling God what is on our hearts, and we're asking God to reveal His will to us. Again in the letter to the Romans, Paul wrote, "... and He who searches the hearts knows

---

29 Romans 1:10
30 Romans 15:32

what the mind of the Spirit is, because He intercedes for the saints according to the *will of God*" (emphasis mine).[31]

Stop right there! You may have just skimmed over something absolutely life changing. Think about that for a moment.

When you pray, the Spirit of God who is in you causes you to pray for the things God wants to accomplish both in and through you. It is for this very reason that prayer is such an intricate aspect of discerning God's will. To not pray is to say, effectively, that you really don't want God's will done in your life—that you couldn't care less.

Question: How is your prayer life right now?

When you pray to God, the Spirit of God works in your life, unfolding His plan right before your very eyes. But what I also find interesting is that sometimes our prayers are the very means God uses to disclose His will in other people's lives as well. Yes, that's correct. God uses you and your prayers to help the people around you understand His plan for their own lives.

While writing to the Colossian Christians, Paul told them, "Epaphras, who is one of your number, a bondslave of Jesus Christ, sends you his greetings, always laboring earnestly for you in his prayers, that you may stand perfect and fully assured in all the *will of God*" (emphasis mine).[32] One critical element for discerning God's will is that you also pray for the people in your own local church assembly. That is God's plan for you and the local church

---

31 Romans 8:27
32 Colossians 4:12

you attend for fellowship. God wants you to be a prayer warrior, both for yourself and for others.

GOD'S WILL IS THAT YOU BE INVOLVED IN MINISTRY

When a person is saved, sanctified, repentant, thankful, and prayerful, the obvious result is that such a man or woman will be faithfully serving others in ministry. Show me a Christian not involved in any ministry, and we'll both be staring at someone depressed spiritually. There are no lone-ranger Christians in your local assembly. Every one of God's children is to be actively involved in ministering to the needs of others around them. Such is the will of God for you and your local church.

When teaching on spiritual gifts and how they're to be used in serving others, the apostle Paul wrote about how a renewed mind—not conformed to the world's desires— leads to the proving of God's will in a person's life. He wrote, "And do not be conformed to this world, but be transformed by the renewing of your mind, so that you may prove what the *will of God* is, that which is good and acceptable and perfect" (emphasis mine).[33] To be conformed to the world is to practice sinful things. To renew your mind is the sanctifying transformation that proves God's will. And God says that this is both acceptable and perfect in His sight.

There was a time when the apostle Paul was warned about going back to Jerusalem to do ministry because it would lead to his imprisonment. Yet Paul would not be

---

33 Romans 12:2

persuaded to do anything other than proclaim the gospel to the city of Jerusalem. When those who were with Paul knew his mind was set, "since he would not be persuaded, we fell silent, remarking, 'The *will of the Lord* be done!'" (emphasis mine)[34]

Maybe today you're wondering about this very issue. Perhaps you've been praying about which ministry to dive into, where to serve geographically, or whom you should serve. Or maybe you have been serving faithfully in a particular ministry, but you believe the Lord is now leading you to minister somewhere else and in some other capacity. My advice to you would be to just start moving. Yes, get moving! The Lord will direct your steps. If God closes the door in one area of your life, He'll open a window somewhere else. God wants you ministering to people, for that's precisely why He empowered you with supernatural spiritual gifts in the first place. He wants you to be overwhelmingly successful in ministry.

Paul and his traveling missionary companions once encountered similar challenges when trying to figure out God's will for their ministry. They had prayed about a location and planned to go there to share the gospel and plant some churches, but one thing after another prevented them from getting there. "They passed through the Phrygian and Galatian region, having been forbidden by the Holy Spirit to speak the word in Asia; and after they came to Mysia, they were trying to go into Bithynia, and the Spirit of Jesus did not permit them; and passing by Mysia, they came down to Troas. A vision appeared to Paul in the night:

---

34 Acts 21:14

a man of Macedonia was standing and appealing to him, and saying, 'Come over to Macedonia and help us.' When he had seen the vision, immediately we sought to go into Macedonia, concluding that God had called us to preach the gospel to them."[35]

Such is the mind of the Lord. God works in both strange and mysterious ways. I'm not saying God will grant you a vision in the middle of night, but I do know that when you set out to minister to others for the glory of God, He will most certainly direct your steps. Ministry is God's plan. It is His plan for your life today.

GOD'S WILL IS THAT YOU BE A GIVING PERSON

The people of God are people who give their resources back to God and His people. Everything you have received comes down from your heavenly Father, and so God wants you to be marked as a person who cheerfully gives.

Writing about the many churches throughout Macedonia, the apostle Paul boasted that they were an extremely giving bunch of saints. "For I testify that according to their ability, and beyond their ability, they gave of their own accord, begging us with much urging for the favor of participation in the support of the saints, and this, not as we had expected, but they first gave themselves to the Lord and to us by the *will of God*" (emphasis mine).[36] God's will for you is to labor in giving of yourself, your time, and your resources, so that others would be blessed and God would be glorified.

---

35 Acts 16:6–10
36 2 Corinthians 8:3–5

Question: Who do you know that is in great need at this moment? Yes, as in right now. This very moment. What can you give, supply, or offer in order to meet that need? It is God's will that you do.

GOD'S WILL IS THAT YOU BE SUBMISSIVE

Another important area of your life where God has specifically revealed His will is regarding your need to be submissive. Rather than be bossy, domineering, or self-seeking, Christians are to be submissive, both to one another and to the government ruling over them.

In today's contemporary American society, there are some Christians who place a rather unhealthy emphasis on politics or social issues, to the detriment of both the gospel and their own personal testimony. At the same time, however, there are far too many Christians who are of the mindset that Christians should have little or nothing to do with politics altogether. Both groups, I believe, would do well to reconsider their position according to what the Scriptures teach. Indeed, God has an opinion about this very issue as well.

God's desire for you is that you "submit yourselves for the Lord's sake to every human institution, whether to a king as the one in authority, or to governors as sent by him for the punishment of evildoers and the praise of those who do right. For such is the *will of God* that by doing right you may silence the ignorance of foolish men. Act as free men, and do not use your freedom as a covering for evil, but use

it as bondslaves of God. Honor all people, love the brother-
hood, fear God, honor the king" (emphasis mine).[37]

Submission to government (and higher authority) is
important to God, because there is no government in existence that is not ordained by God. Some governments
prove to be both cruel and unusually brutal, but each
person in authority will give an account of their actions to
their Creator come Judgment Day. Your responsibility is to
be in submission to whichever government you find yourself under at the moment. For American Christians, this
could change every four years or so.

Americans are governed by the Constitution of the
United States and not, necessarily, by whoever sits in the
oval office come Election Day. Ours is a government of
the people, by the people, and for the people. Under this
political system of democracy, we are granted certain rights
and responsibilities. We have the freedom of speech, the
right to assemble, and the right to vote. Therefore, to insist
that all Christians should remove themselves from politics
altogether is a gross error and, frankly, goes against God's
revealed will to be submissive to our American government. If there ever comes a time when you personally find
yourself under the rule of a different government, then
God's desire for you is to be submissive to that authority,
do what is right, silence ignorant men by nothing more
than your exemplary behavior, respect everyone around
you, love other believers, and honor the king.

So long as the governing authorities are not demanding
that we do anything God has specifically forbidden, or

---

37 1 Peter 2:13-17

requires us to refrain from doing something God has specifically commanded us to do, we are to always submit. Submission is God's revealed will for your life.

GOD'S WILL IS THAT YOU BE A HARD WORKER

Many people don't enjoy their jobs, the people they work with, or the boss they report to. But another area God has specifically revealed His will about is the area of voluntary employment, indentured servitude, and outright slavery. If you ever find yourself a slave—the owned possession of a harsh slave master—then God's will is that you work ever so diligently on their behalf. This is a hard one, I admit. With the idea of slavery in mind, however, how much greater workers should we be as voluntary employees?

Writing to the church in Ephesus, the apostle Paul said, "Slaves, be obedient to those who are your masters according to the flesh, with fear and trembling, in the sincerity of your heart, as to Christ; not by way of eyeservice, as men-pleasers, but as slaves of Christ, doing the *will of God* from the heart. With good will render service, as to the Lord, and not to men, knowing that whatever good thing each one does, this he will receive back from the Lord, whether slave or free" (emphasis mine).[38] I don't know about you, but this one is hard for me to swallow!

Under the inspiration of the Holy Spirit, Paul says that when you work, act like your boss—your slave master—is Jesus Christ Himself.

---

38 Ephesians 6:5-8

Question: Would you follow the demands and expectations of your employer more closely if your boss was Jesus
Christ Himself? Most of us would probably answer yes,
which means that we've likely broken this command for
God's will in our lives. The service we each render as
an employee is to be faithful, giving one hundred per-
cent of our time, attention, and motivation to our master's
(employer's) business.

It may seem difficult—even unreasonable at times—to
do this, but it is, nevertheless, God's revealed will for you.
When it comes to your job, God wants you performing
the will of the Lord from the heart, from 8 a.m. to 5 p.m.,
Monday through Friday, and even during overtime.

GOD'S WILL IS THAT YOU BE WISE, NOT FOOLISH

God is no fool, and His children aren't to be foolish
either. God's design for His children is that we be wise,
not foolish. To be foolish is to do something other than
what is the obvious and correct choice.

For example, walking against oncoming traffic on an
interstate highway is foolish. You're going to die—it's just a
matter of time. It's not a wise thing to do. Likewise, jumping
off the roof of a thirty-story building in order to test the
theory of gravity would be a foolish thing to do. Again,
you're going to die if you do that. It isn't wise. And God
doesn't want His children to be marked as a foolish people.

We are all fools for Christ's sake, certainly, but that's
the world's general assessment of us due to our faith in an
unseen God. But God's assessment of the situation is quite

different. In fact, it would seem from Scripture that to *not* understand God's will for your life is actually indicative of foolishness itself!

Did you catch that? To not rightly discern God's basic will for your life is a display of flippant folly.

It isn't as though God is sitting on His throne in giggles, entertaining Himself by hiding critical bits and pieces of His plan from you. Nor is the Lord's will like the proverbial carrot on a string: close enough to be interesting, but not close enough to be tasted. No! The Scripture says, "So then do not be foolish, but understand what the *will of the Lord* is" (emphasis mine).[39]

Yes, the Lord wants you to both know and readily act upon His plan for your life. He wants you saved, sanctified, thankful, sexually pure, submissive, and wise.

Question: How are you doing so far with this list of God's revealed plan for your life?

GOD'S WILL IS FOR YOU TO BE GOD-CENTERED

Another area of your life that may need to be refocused is your God-centeredness. Are you worldly-minded or Christ-exalting? Are you consumed with the pursuit of meaningless things, or are you passionate about being God-centered in every aspect of your life? It is God's will that you be so heavenly-focused.

The apostle John wrote, "The world is passing away, and also its lusts; but the one who does the *will of God*

---

39 Ephesians 5:17

lives forever" (emphasis mine).[40] The unregenerate people of this world are marked by lust and greed. They long for the husks of the world. Their end is the way of destruction. God's people, on the other hand, will live forever. To be God-centered, then, is to be singularly focused on praising His name, exalting the Savior, and spreading the gospel. Everything in this world is moving toward decay and destruction, but if you are one of God's adopted children, then you are to be consciously living for the glory of God.

GOD'S WILL IS THAT YOU MAY BE SUFFERING

Of all the verses dealing with God's specific plan for your life, this one is no doubt the toughest to embrace. It just may be that God's will for your life is not what you might personally consider a *wonderful* plan. It very well could be that God's desire for you is to suffer. And suffer long without an end in sight.

The apostle Peter wrote, "Therefore, those also who suffer according to the *will of God* shall entrust their souls to a faithful Creator in doing what is right" (emphasis mine).[41] I know: ouch! If you're anything like me, this isn't anything close to what you had in mind regarding God's plan for your life.

I prefer pleasure to pain, happiness to sadness, and acceptance when compared to rejection. Most people do, and for obvious reasons. But there are times when God prefers that His children endure a time of pain rather than a season of

---

40 1 John 2:17
41 1 Peter 4:19

pleasure, sadness instead of happiness, and flat-out rejection by those around them. When you endure severe hardship—maintaining your integrity all the way through it—God receives a great wealth of glory, and you're building up a spiritual prize that He will dole out when the time is right, whether in this life or the next.

I don't know about you, but when I think of God's children suffering painfully, I often think of a woman named Joni Eareckson Tada.

In 1967, at the age of seventeen, Joni was injured in a diving accident that left her a quadriplegic in a wheelchair. No doubt there were many lonely nights in which Joni spent by herself and with no one other than God. And there were likely many times when she would ask questions like, "Why me, God?" or "Why did you let this happen to me?" But as one looks back at Joni's life since that life-altering day of paralysis, you can't help but notice how often God has used her to be a tremendous blessing to others.

Joni has authored over seventy books, served on the National Council on Disability under President Reagan and President Bush, and more recently on the Disability Advisory Committee to the U.S. State Department under Secretary of State Condoleezza Rice. But as impressive a resume as that is, there are untold thousands (maybe millions?) of common folk who have been helped, encouraged, and ministered to by the positive outlook on life that Joni so eloquently models. She has a heart for hurting people and grieves right alongside those in desperate need. I don't think it's a stretch to say that it is highly unlikely she would have ever been used in the capacity she has obviously been used by God in, if she hadn't had that terrible diving accident in 1967.

God works in mysterious ways, indeed.

When God's children suffer, God also feels the pain. When Jesus was nailed to the cross for your sin, God the Father also felt the nail's sting. Jesus endured God's wrath for you. God understands your pain and anxiety, and He will never leave you nor forsake you. But there are both strange and hard-to-understand times when God's plan is for you to suffer.

Down through the centuries, millions of God's people have been murdered, enslaved, and viciously beaten, due to nothing more than their uncompromising Christian faith. But suffering comes in many different shapes and sizes, and not all suffering is created equal.

Many Christian men, for example, have lost their jobs because they refused to lie, cheat, or steal on behalf of their employer, and many of these same men went through tremendous stress trying to secure another job. Moreover, many godly women have endured ridicule by family, friends and media for choosing to stay at home with the kids rather than getting a "real" job. Yes, there are many kinds of suffering that God's people must endure, and not all of it is physical. Emotional, mental, and psychological suffering takes place all the time among the people who know Jesus Christ as their Brother.

But make no mistake about it, when you suffer as a Christian, you are entrusting your soul to a faithful Creator who will never leave or forsake you. He has your name written down in His Book of Life. Your acceptance is engraved on His hands. You will always be a part of God's plan, for all eternity to come. It is His plan for you.

GOD'S WILL IS THAT YOU DO WHATEVER YOU WANT

How many times have you personally prayed for the knowledge of God's will? Twenty times? Fifty? Five hundred? Maybe even more than that? It's weird how we often ask for things we already possess, and for things God would freely give us if we planned to use them appropriately. Here's what I mean by that.

I have five children at the moment, and my two oldest are boys. Boys, in case you don't know, are quite different from girls. Every once in a while my boys and I will go through some cabinets or boxes, looking for this or that, and we'll stumble upon a gadget I haven't used in years. Some time ago, one of my sons found my old portable CD player, which by today's standards is rather outdated technology. But he thought it was cool and wanted to play with it. I put some new batteries in it and away he went. An hour or two later, he walked up to me with all of his money in hand.

"Dad, I want to buy your CD player," he said.

"No, it's okay, you can keep playing with it. I won't charge you anything for using it," I replied, smiling.

"But I want it. How much would you sell it to me for?"

"I don't want to sell it to you. You can use it whenever you want to."

"Yes, I know, but I want it to be mine. How about $5? Will $5 be enough?"

"No, I don't want your money. There's no reason for me to sell it to you. You live in this house and you can use it," I said, smiling a lot less at this point.

"But I really like it and I want to own it. I want to keep it in my room and use it whenever I want to. How much, Dad?"

It was around this point in the conversation that I said, "Hmm, I think I'd like $100 for it. How much do you have? Not quite enough, huh? Well, you can't play with it then. It's mine. Sorry. Come back when you have enough money. You've got to pay to play, kid." And then I took the CD player away from him.

Well, my son was not at all happy. Or amused. I then told him to look me in the eyes. When he did, I said, "Son, I am not interested in taking your money. You belong to me, and if I want to let you or your brothers and sisters use something of mine, I will not expect to be paid for it. When you keep trying to pay me for it, what you're basically telling me is, 'I don't believe you, Dad. I don't believe that you'll just let me have it. I think you'll take it away from me when I'm not looking. But if I buy it outright, then I don't need to worry about you anymore.'"

I then asked my son how he thought that made me feel. He confessed that it would make me feel sad, and I agreed.

You see, I think we do that far too often with God too. God wants us to know His will, to be completely informed about His plan for our life, to not be foolish, and to do what is right. He doesn't need us negotiating with Him or trying to manipulate the situation by saying, "Oh, I'll do this-and-that if You'll let me know Your will for my life in this area."

Yes, I think God gets rather annoyed when we do that. Don't you?

THE MOMENT OF TRUTH FOR YOU

Here's the great news of this chapter. Ready? Just do whatever you want to do!

If you want to go to a particular college, then apply, get accepted, pack your bags, and go. If you want to get another job, then do what you can to find a new and adequate job, and once you've found it, take it!

Look, if you are being obedient to God in the things listed above, then I've got news for you—you're in God's will right now! Just start moving in the direction you want to go, and God will direct your steps. He won't allow you to stumble.

If you are saved, sanctified, repentant, thankful, prayerful, sexually pure, involved in ministry, giving, submissive, a good employee, wise and not foolish, God-centered, and willing to suffer for His glory, then do whatever you want to. That's right, do whatever you want! If you are doing everything you can to live a godly life, to serve others, and glorify God in whatever you say and do, then just start moving. God will open a door so wide for you that you could drive a bus through it.

It really is that simple.

If your heart, mind, soul, and strength are completely tuned into God's glory, then He will give you the desires of your heart. He will do so because your desires would be centered on His glory. And that's precisely what He wants for you in the first place!

Pastor John MacArthur put it this way: "Keep moving—what a principle! So many people sit around waiting for that celestial crane to move them and saying, 'I don't know what God wants me to do.' They need to start moving so God can steer them to that area of service He has planned. Knowing God's will may mean pushing down a narrow line until you hit a dead end. At that point, God will open a door so wide, you won't be able to see around it—only through it!"[42]

FIRST THINGS FIRST

At this point you may be thinking something like, *That sounds way too easy, Charles. What's the catch?* And my answer would be that there isn't a catch. You just need to be progressively obedient in each of the areas listed above. That's what God has revealed to you.

And so, if you're not saved, then don't assume for a minute that such a notion would ever work for you.

If you're saved, but really not all that concerned about being sanctified, then God's will is unlikely to work itself out for you.

If you're saved, but not praying, then don't hold your breath. (That's right, don't hold your breath!)

If you're promoting a fake, external façade of public godliness, but privately you're sexually immoral or indulging in internet pornography, then again—don't hold your

---

42 John MacArthur, <u>Found: God's Will</u> (David C. Clark, 1977), page 59.

breath. God's will has already been revealed in Scripture, and He's not about to give you more of what you're currently unwilling to swallow.

If you're saved, thankful, sexually pure, submissive, but not involved in any real ministry, then again, don't hold your breath. There's no way God will reveal more when you've rejected the first fruits of His plan for your life.

"You see," John MacArthur wrote, "the will of God is not primarily a place. The will of God is not, first of all, for you to go there or work here. The will of God concerns you as a person. If you are the right you, you can follow your desires and you will fulfill His will."[43]

Question: How are you doing with these? Are you the sort of person God wants you to be?

- Are you saved?

- Are you diligently pursuing progressive sanctification?

- Are you repentant and thankful?

- Are you praying without ceasing?

- Are you sexually pure?

- Are you involved in ministry, serving others?

- Are you a giving and submissive person?

- Are you a productive worker?

- Are you wise and God-centered?

---

43 *Ibid*, page 60.

- Are you willing to suffer if that's God's plan for your life?

If these areas of your life are at all lacking what they should be, then get it together! It's God's will that you do.

CHAPTER FOUR

God's Will: Uncompromising Worship

"'Teacher, which is the great commandment in the Law?' And He said to him, 'You shall love the LORD your God with all your heart, and with all your soul, and with all your mind.'" (Matthew 22:36-37)

"Missions is not the ultimate goal of the church. Worship is. Missions exists because worship doesn't. Worship is ultimate, not missions, because God is ultimate, not man. When this age is over, and the countless millions of the redeemed fall on their faces before the throne of God, missions will be no more. It is a temporary necessity. But worship abides forever." –John Piper

I T WAS A gorgeous Saturday morning, and I was feeling especially creative. Rather chef-like. For some crazy reason I got the idea in my head that I should cook breakfast for everyone in the house. If you've heard anything about my notorious culinary skills, then you'll understand this was a bad idea.

Not wanting to be overly ambitious, I decided on making pancakes. Simple pancakes. I grabbed one of my wife's cookbooks and opened to the cake section. It had a picture of a stack of puffy hotcakes along with an easy-to-follow recipe. Perfect.

After grabbing the largest bowl in the kitchen, I started adding in the ingredients. Water...check! Flour...check! Eggs...check! I then came to the point where I needed to add about two teaspoons of baking powder. Powder? I must have searched the kitchen drawers for about ten minutes looking for something called *baking powder*. No luck. I thought to myself, *It's only a little powder anyway. Surely it won't matter if I leave it out altogether.* And so I did. By the time I had finished adding in all the ingredients, I left out the baking powder and substituted a couple of other ingredients for things easier to find in our pantry.

So far, so good.

As soon as I poured the batter onto the griddle, however, I knew something was wrong. My pancakes were paper-thin and were actually shiny. Shiny?

Awakened by the noxious fumes floating around the house, my wife strolled into the kitchen and proceeded to laugh at my culinary creation.

"Why are they so flat...and shiny?" she asked. I explained what I'd done. She then proceeded to grab her camera and started taking pictures. Her laughter awoke all our children, and after seeing their father's attempt at making breakfast, they said, "We're not eating those. They look poisonous!"

Undeterred by all the mockery, I vowed to personally eat all the pancakes in order to demonstrate just how tasty they were. Unfortunately, they looked a lot better than they tasted. No amount of maple syrup would help, either. I think I forced down two small bites before chucking it into the trash.

That morning I learned two important life-lessons. The first lesson is that it's safer just to go out and buy a dozen donuts for breakfast. The second lesson I learned is that quite often it's the seemingly insignificant things in life that end up being the most important in the end.

This is true, both in making breakfast and in figuring out God's will for your life.

PUTTING THE CART BEFORE THE HORSE

Perspective is everything. Don't ever lose sight of the fact that your role in Christianity is not about motivating scores of Christians to get up and go evangelize the world. That is not our primary purpose. It is an important ingredient to the discipleship recipe—to be sure—but getting believers motivated about evangelism is a lower-tiered objective.

Remember, the local church's mission in this world is to *make disciples of Jesus Christ*, not merely to *go*.

As believers, we so want to see God turn sinners away from the vain worship of idols and become disciples of the true and living God. Our desire is to behold the Lord Jesus Christ save a people for Himself, lifting the veil of unbelief from the eyes of poor wretches. That is our sole aim, our singular purpose, and our main goal for ministry. The act of *going out* into the nations with the gospel is essentially our supernatural response to the Master's plan of discipleship. We go, trusting in the Lord that He alone will make the disciples.

Yet even that, I believe, fails miserably at painting the true masterpiece of what our heart's desire should be in fulfilling Great Commission Discipleship. The imperative verb in the Great Commission mandate is *make* disciples, yes, but our ultimate goal for discipleship should never be that shallow. It is a glorious blessing to behold the Lord build His Church, but our primary motivation for ministry should not even be to save sinners from the pits of Hell. Our motivation for ministry and discipleship, however, should certainly be to love and worship the God who saves!

FOCUSING ON WHAT MATTERS MOST

Worshipping God is a believer's ultimate end, not to mention our beginning and middle and everything else in between. Great Commission Discipleship is simply the means by which worship of the divine Trinity is our end.

In answering a question about what the motive for evangelism should be, J.I. Packer wrote, "There are, in fact, two motives that should spur us constantly to evangelize. The first is love to God and concern for His glory; the second is love to man and concern for his welfare."[44]

If your focus in ministry inhibits God-centered worship, then whatever sits upon the throne of your motivation becomes a two-faced idol. If our ministries are all

---

44 J.I. Packer, Evangelism & the Sovereignty of God (InterVarsity Press, 1961), page 73.

about getting other people to *go*, and not primarily about worshipping God through loving obedience to His commandments, then we have failed even before we've begun. The ministries of evangelism and discipleship would have become a two-faced idol.

Mark Dever wrote, "...our love for people can prove inadequate. The motivating force for our whole life, including evangelism, must be our love for God."[45] So if our *sole* compulsion is to make disciples of Jesus Christ while being thoroughly involved in ministry and service, we may impress men...but God is not amused.

DO NOT LEAVE YOUR FIRST LOVE

Failing to love God is the very heart of all sin. It was also the main problem addressed in the letter Jesus sent to the church at Ephesus in Revelation 2:1-7.

The apostle Paul was instrumental in founding the Ephesian church, and he pastored there for about three years.[46] Both Timothy and Tychicus ministered there from time to time, and the apostle John himself ministered in and around Ephesus until he was arrested and banished to the Island of Patmos.

That cluster of Ephesian Christians had a long line of rock-solid leadership and rich doctrine. Even Jesus Himself confessed that they "cannot tolerate evil men, and you put to the test those who call themselves apostles, and they are not, and you found them to be false."[47] As if that wasn't

---

45 Mark Dever, The Gospel & Personal Evangelism (Crossway Books, 2007), page 100.
46 See Acts 19, 20
47 Revelation 2:2

impressive enough, the dust never settled on that flock of believers, either. Armed with godly leadership and sound theology, the church went into their local community and administered the gospel on a regular basis.

It seemed as though the Ephesian church had hit the bull's-eye of God's will regarding what most churches strive for today: sound doctrine and active participation in ministry.

Jesus didn't fail to take notice of that fact, either. He acknowledged their admirable affection toward ministry, saying, "I know your deeds and your toil and perseverance."[48] Our Lord had no quarrel with their commitment to Scripture or ministry, commending both their hard work and tireless attitude. What Jesus did find revolting, however, was the fact that they had vetoed any love for Him! That was the error of their Christianity. Jesus complimented their heresy-free theology and perseverance in ministry; He just didn't want to be ignored while it all took place.

What offended God was that they brandished "successful" ministries, yet possessed little affection for the Savior. They had abandoned their first love. Imagine—Christianity with no love for Christ. Godliness with no passion for God. Absurd! They studied and toiled in ministry, yet lost sight of their primary objective: worship.

Knowledge of God's holy Word should have led them to a more radical love for Jesus, but it did not. Perseverance in ministry should have been the supernatural response to their passionate love of the Savior, but it was not. And because this was the extent of their cold and shallow

48 *Ibid.*

orthodoxy, Jesus had little more than a stiff rebuke for that church as a whole.

He said, "Therefore remember from where you have fallen, and repent and do the deeds you did at first; or else I am coming to you and will remove your lampstand out of its place—unless you repent."[49] To put it another way, Jesus was essentially telling them, "I will close the doors of your church forever if you don't make love for Me the motivation for both your pursuit of theology and ministry toward others."

WHAT DOES GOD REALLY WANT FROM YOU?

It is amazing, really, how totally unconcerned Jesus is about the number of churches there are in a given city. Or even the number of people in a particular congregation, for that matter. Worship is always the target, never popularity. Frankly, this is what many in American Christianity need to be reminded of today as well, regarding God's will for both them personally and their local church. And soon, too, before their lampstand gets permanently removed once and for all.

Great Commission Discipleship is exciting work and promises tremendous blessings to those who walk by faith, teaching right doctrine in their course of going. But don't be so foolish as to think you can accomplish anything to make God smile unless love for Jesus is the driving force for everything in your spiritual walk—including ministry. To think otherwise could lead, as with Ephesus, to the demise of your local assembly.

---

49 Revelation 2:5

Sadly, I believe this may be the very reason why many churches across America and beyond do not prosper and must, therefore, close their doors for good. They may have had solid theology and a gripping ministry or two, but it's quite possible that Jesus would have felt uncomfortable sitting in their pews. I may very well be wrong in many cases, but I am saddened to think I could be right on target with some.

Beloved, do not lose sight of your passionate love for Jesus Christ. This is most certainly God's revealed will for your life today.

THE BENEFITS OF THOROUGH SELF-EXAMINATION

Remember Mark? In Acts 15:36-41 we read about Mark, a young guy who initially failed at keeping the worship of God his main priority. He took his eyes off the Lord and focused his attention on things that dragged him off the path of radical discipleship. No doubt he knew that the right thing to do was worship God with an uncompromising and subservient heart, but for a time he took his eyes off that holy prize.

We all do this from time to time. Life sometimes feels more like an up-and-down rollercoaster than anything resembling consistency. God is so gracious to us when we fail Him. His mercy is so wonderfully abundant.

The apostle Paul concluded this fact about Mark, and it led to a boxing match between Barnabas and himself. "Paul kept insisting that they should not take him along who had deserted them in Pamphylia and had not gone with them to the work."[50] Paul refused to allow Mark to tag along on a mission trip because his priorities were not in line with what the ministry required. As far as Paul was concerned, Mark had become useless to them in ministry. Altogether useless! Rather than uncompromising worship, Mark longed for a more *comfortable* Christianity. The issue became so serious that it caused Paul and Barnabas to part ways and minister in opposite directions of one another. Paul grabbed Silas and went off in one direction while Mark trailed behind Barnabas in the opposite.

Yet praise the Lord that He remains the God of second chances!

Sometime later, Mark refocused his calling to Great Commission Discipleship and placed the priority of worshipping God back as his ultimate motivation for ministry. It was only then that Paul was willing to write to Timothy, saying, "Pick up Mark and bring him with you, for he is useful to me for service."[51]

God will use any man, woman, or child, as long as they are sold out to the praise of His glory alone.

Question: Are you sold out to the uncompromising worship of God Almighty, or are you holding hands with the world?

THE CHURCH IS NOT A TEMP AGENCY

When Jesus walked the earth, preaching in such a manner that the multitudes were constantly in awe, He was also careful to set aside time to teach His disciples privately. On

---

50 Acts 15:38
51 2 Timothy 4:11

one occasion He did this and focused specifically on evangelism, which is illuminated further for us today since we can evaluate this teaching in light of the Great Commission.

Upon appointing the seventy disciples to go into the cities ahead of Him, Jesus said, "The harvest is plentiful, but the laborers are few; therefore beseech the Lord of the harvest to send out laborers into His harvest."[52] Notice that although Jesus does say we should pray that the Lord would raise up laborers to go, He places the emphasis not on the laborers themselves, but on the Lord and His abundant harvest. The focus is to always be centered on God, never on us.

There is a great white harvest of souls out there to be reaped, gathered, and discipled, but precious few are willing to wield the sickle of radical obedience. There are disciples yet to be *made*, but the vast majority of those *already* made are unwilling to get their hands dirty in the Lord's garden.

WALKING WORTHY OF THE LORD

I recently read a story about a Christian convert from Burma who was brought to America and asked to speak at a conference regarding the local church's responsibility to send out missionaries around the world. After a moment of deep thought, and with a fair amount of confusion, he finally asked, "Has not Christ told you to do it?" "Oh yes," was the reply, "but we wish you to remind them of their duty." "Oh, no," said the Karen honestly, "if they will not mind Jesus, they will not mind me!"[53] How very true.

Great Commission Discipleship is about glorifying

---

52 Luke 10:2
53 MoreIllustrations.com, www.moreillustrations.com/Illustrations/
obedience%201.html (accessed January 4, 2013).

God through spiritual duplication. When Jesus commanded the Great Commission as recorded in Matthew 28:19-20, He said to "go...and make disciples...baptizing them...teaching them to observe all that I commanded you." You see, the will of God is found first in being taught to obey what Christ has already revealed (commanded).

In other words, Christians are always on the go. While on the go, we make others into disciples of Jesus Christ. Once a disciple is made, they're to be baptized and taught God's Word. The "made" disciple is fed essential doctrines and sound theology ("all that I commanded you") and encouraged to passionately "observe" (obey) those things in every facet of life.

In other words, the baptized and catechized disciples are expected to live out the theology they are being taught day-by-day (a mind-blowing concept, I know). A significant portion of such obedience in your daily life is to evangelize the lost by living for the glory of God. To observe all that Christ commanded you is to be entrenched in the process of going (daily obedience). We see, then, that Great Commission Discipleship is a circular, never-ending process of spiritual duplication.

Scripture is so marvelously clear that if a churchgoer refuses to obey God's will and go, then they're disobeying the biblical truths they're being taught. A blatant willingness to disregard God's Word is sinful. Christians who willfully disobey God in the essential truths of Scripture should never expect God to reveal further things about His will for their life. If a churchgoer willingly continues in a patterned lifestyle of disobedience in not sharing his faith and/or growing in the knowledge of the truth, then his faith is suspect at best. He could hardly be described as a genuinely made disciple of Jesus Christ.

THE PRICE TAG OF KNOWING GOD'S WILL

When Jesus informed the disciples that they would be His "witnesses both in Jerusalem, and in Judea and Samaria, and even to the remotest part of the earth," I'm convinced they were clueless and had no idea about the immensity of that Great Commission statement.[54] I will address their ignorance of the geographic segment of God's will in a later chapter, but for now let's focus on what Jesus meant when He said they would be His witnesses.

The word translated "witnesses" in Acts 1:8 is the Greek word "martures," from which we get our English word "martyrs." To be a biblical witness for Jesus Christ, then, means being a martyr.

Many of the early Christians (and millions more still today) were tortured and murdered for their unwavering commitment to Jesus Christ. They were speared, crucified, stoned, sawn in half, boiled in oil, thrown to the wild beasts for blood-thirsty sport, set on fire as human torches for entertainment purposes, and otherwise met their end at the hands of one medieval device or another. Their public and unabashed profession of faith proved to be the basis for their persecution.

Our beloved brothers and sisters in Christ weren't murdered because they loved their neighbor or refused to lie, cheat, or steal—and they didn't have their lives snuffed

---

54 Acts 1:8

out because of their generosity in sharing their possessions with the poor, either. The breath of life was snatched from their lungs because they publicly verbalized an unrelenting faith they had in a crucified and resurrected Messiah.

IN LIFE AND DEATH

All around the globe Christians today are still witnesses for the Lord Jesus Christ. If you're a Christian, then you are a martyr for the sake of Christ. It has been estimated that "an average of 171,000 Christians worldwide are martyred for their faith per year."[55] According to *The Voice of the Martyrs*, in a 2009 report in the International Bulletin of Missionary Research, researchers estimated that there were approximately "160,000 martyrs in mid-2000 and 34,000 at the beginning of the 20th century. If current trends continue...by 2025, an average of 210,000 Christians will be martyred annually."[56]

Those are certainly troubling statistics, but they're also more than mere statistics. Those numbers represent our brothers and sisters in Christ. Lord willing, this doesn't mean you will literally be killed for your faith in the Lord who purchased you, but it very well could. However, if your life ever does come to that transcendent crossroad, are you willing to hold fast your faith, no matter the cost?

Consider the great apostle Peter for a moment. After reinstating Peter and calling him to the ministry of tending God's sheep, Jesus then revealed that the day would

---

55 About.com, www.Christianity.about.com/od/denominations/p/ christiantoday.htm (accessed January 4, 2013).
56 The Voice of the Martyrs, www.persecutedchurch.blogspot.com/2009/04/ limits-of-statistics.html (accessed January 4, 2013).

soon arrive for the apostle to be murdered for his faith, likely by crucifixion. The apostle's martyrdom was part of God's revealed plan for Peter to glorify Him, even in death. Immediately after Jesus predicted Peter's death, the Scripture says, "Now this He said, signifying by what kind of death he would *glorify God*" (emphasis mine).[57]

Most Christians don't want to hear that. I don't like thinking about it myself. But martyrs, you see, both live and die for the glory of God. There are no other options available to us. Living and dying for God's glory is His revealed will for our lives.

Question: Who are you living for right now? Are you living for the glory of God or for the glory of the god called *Self*? What is your life's purpose here in this world? What are you willing to die for? More importantly, what are you willing to live for? If God chose to take your life so that He would receive glory in your martyrdom—and He told you all about it before it happened—would you be furious or thankful?

Our lives are truly a mist, and if God so wills that your or my vapor vanishes in order to manifest His magnificent glory, our desire should be for nothing less. Yes, it's certainly hard to maintain such an outlook in both life and death, but it's the only one acceptable to God. The very worst death can ever do is usher us into God's presence.

Frankly, that sounds rather appealing. Doesn't it?

---

57 John 21:19

DYING DAILY FOR GOD

Regardless of whether or not your life comes to an abrupt halt as a literal martyr for the gospel of Jesus Christ, you need to die daily.

Jesus made that unquestionably clear when He said, "If anyone wishes to come after Me, he must *deny himself*, and take up his cross daily and follow Me" (emphasis mine).[58] Fulfilling God's will is a hard thing to do. It requires patience, stamina, and an uncompromising loyalty to the God who saved you.

In our contemporary culture, the vast majority of American Christians will never be severely harassed for their faith, let alone murdered. Yet we're all commanded to lay down our lives day-by-day. That is your high calling. That is your ministry in this world. That is God's revealed will for your life. It's what it means to go and be a passionate witness to all the nations. You need to die daily so that when you interact with the unregenerate sinners around you, it is as if they are interacting directly with the Spirit of God who reigns in you.

But this can only happen if you die daily, laying down your life as a passionate witness in obedience to Great Commission Discipleship.

Question: What about you? Are you willing to live for God like that? Do you really want God's will to be done in your life? There are no fence-straddlers when it comes to obeying God's will.

---

58 Luke 9:23

Outrageously Expensive,
But So Worth It

Recently I was reading *Foxe's Book of Martyrs*, and as a result I've been both appalled and challenged in my witness for Jesus Christ. Foxe recounts for us a brief biography about a young man's faith that is not only graphic, but also rather convicting.

Some 1,800 years after the fatal event, Christians today are still being encouraged by the testimony of that young man. Foxe tells us, "Agapetus, a boy of Praeneste, in Italy, who was only fifteen years of age, refusing to sacrifice to the idols, was severely scourged and then hanged up by the feet, and boiling water poured over him. He was afterwards worried by wild beasts, and at last beheaded."[59]

Wow! I certainly wouldn't want to experience the torments of Agapetus' final hour, but is that a powerful testimony or what? That teenager, who today would probably be a sophomore in most high schools across America, refused to offer a pinch of incense to a pathetic monarch, and so gladly exchanged the comforts of this world for a house made without hands. He chose to be worried by wild beasts rather than stand worried before his Lord.

A few years back, there was a popular television commercial with an advertisement about Michael Jordan. The commercial encouraged people to "Be like Mike." Actually, I think we should "Be like Agapetus."

Another heart-wrenching account about how the Lord

---

59 John Foxe, <u>Foxes' Book of Martyrs</u> (Ambassador Productions Ltd., 2002), page 14.

used clay pots as His instruments to save sinners was also penned in Foxe's book:

> During the martyrdom of Faustinus and Jovita, brothers and citizens of Brescia, their torments were so many, and their patience so firm, that Calocerius, a pagan, beholding them, was struck with admiration, and exclaimed in ecstasy, 'Great is the God of the Christians!' for which he was apprehended and put to death.[60]

We serve a mighty God. If we American Christians would commit ourselves to uncompromising discipleship so that God would be honored above all else, He just might cause millions of more pagans to cry out, "Great is the God of the Christians!"

BE LIKE STEPHEN

Stephen became the very first Christian martyr of the early church, as recorded in Acts chapter seven. He may have preferred something completely different in life, perhaps even a quality of life defined more by *comfort* than suffering, but that was God's will for Stephen, nevertheless.

With profound respect and outstanding self-control, Stephen debated with his enemies to the point that they were unable to cope with the wisdom and the Spirit with which he was speaking. In their frustration and unbridled hatred of the Messiah he so passionately served, they "stirred up the people, the elders and the scribes, and they came up to him and dragged him away and brought him before

---

60 *Ibid*, page 11.

the Council."[61] They falsely accused Stephen of blasphemy and of altering the customs of Moses. These were charges he was totally innocent of, but which the Sanhedrin committed almost daily. Yet when confronted with lies about his reputation, the threat of bodily persecution, and the uncertainty of his immediate future, Stephen's resolve to remain a radical witness for Jesus Christ led the Council to see no less than the face of an angel.

PORTRAIT OF A GODLY MAN

Rather than close with an altar call and a few stanzas of *Just As I Am*, Stephen preached a passionate sermon on Israel's history. The climax came when he accused the Sanhedrin of committing blasphemy and being just like their fathers who always murdered the prophets. His words cut deep like daggers, yet his behavior so pleased the Lord that Stephen was granted a rare glimpse of the risen Savior, even while the stones rained down upon his frail frame.

Far from returning the assault of stones with a hail of rebuke, Stephen retaliated with the spiritual fruit of love and self-control. He prayed for the forgiveness of his murderers. The Council raced toward Stephen with gnashing teeth and lawless intentions, but all Stephen could do was petition God for their salvation. As stone after stone sliced through the air and met its fatal mark, the resolve of that godly man was to do nothing less than cry out with a loud voice, "Lord, do not hold this sin against them!"[62]

Rather than vengeance, Stephen prayed for mercy. Such radical love. Such uncompromising focus!

61 Acts 6:12
62 Acts 7:60

Stephen remained faithful, while the faithless "witnesses laid aside their robes at the feet of a young man named Saul."[63] It's likely that Saul of Tarsus (who later became the apostle Paul) was present in the synagogue when Stephen debated with his accusers. But he was certainly present when Stephen preached against the leaders of the Sanhedrin before being driven out of the city to breathe his last breath. And yet, while staring into the hollow face of martyrdom, Stephen never took his eyes off the Lord, remaining faithful to the end.

Through the unimaginable pains of those fatal blows, Stephen begged for the forgiveness of his murderers. His final prayer was that God would forgive the very worst of his enemies. Sometime later, God answered that prayer, at least in the life of one of those present that day. God forgave Saul—the man who would soon become known as the great apostle Paul—the man who held the cloaks of Stephen's accusers and was in hearty agreement with putting him to death.

GOD WORKS IN VERY MYSTERIOUS WAYS

As we commit ourselves to the application of God's will regarding Great Commission Discipleship, God works through our actions and prayers in amazing ways. Only the Lord knows in what capacity Stephen's prayer provoked Him to move in Saul's life with merciful salvation. I suppose we may only know once we get to Paradise. Regardless, however, Stephen's witness was so potent that

---

63 Acts 7:58

REVEALED

God chose to devote a fair amount of Scripture to it, just to tell you the story.

We are rarely more like Jesus than when we're witnessing to unbelievers, for Christ spent so much of His time spreading the gospel among sinners. This is supported by our Lord's own Great Commission words in John 20:21 when He said, "As the Father has sent Me, I also send you." Jesus offered His life as a ransom for many because He refused to allow the comforts of this world to compete against His mission to glorify His Father. Stephen's life and death are reminiscent of that singular devotion as well.

John MacArthur wrote the following words about this godly guy named Stephen:

> Both in life and in death, Stephen was so much like his Lord. Jesus was filled with the Spirit, so was Stephen. Jesus was full of grace, so was Stephen. Jesus boldly confronted the religious establishment of his day, so did Stephen. Jesus was convicted by lying witnesses, so was Stephen. Jesus had a mock trial, so did Stephen. Jesus was executed though innocent of any crime, so was Stephen. Both were accused of blasphemy. Both died outside the city and were buried by sympathizers. And as already noted, both prayed for the salvation of their executioners. Was there ever a man more like Jesus?[64]

Question: What about you? Are you content with being just an average, run-of-the-mill churchgoer, or do you want to become more like Jesus every day? No, I mean do

---

64 John MacArthur, The MacArthur New Testament Commentary, Acts 1-12 (The Moody Bible Institute of Chicago, 1994); page 226.

you *really* want to be Christ-like? There's a big difference, after all. Do you truly want God's will to be done in your life, or are you merely looking for provisional happiness and worldly comforts?

We need to be intentional as we go day-by-day making disciples of all the nations. That is our chief duty. It is God's revealed will for each of us. Regardless of the impact to your 401k, your reputation, or even your physical body, you need to strive toward uncompromising obedience, passionately worshipping the King of Kings and warning sinners to flee from the wrath to come.

It is the main reason you are here on Earth. It's why you're still inhaling and exhaling right now.

You are an ambassador for the Lord. You've been commissioned with the God-ordained ministry of reconciliation. And fruit-bearing ambassadors earn their living in a foreign land (Earth), far away from the comforts of their true home (Heaven).

CHAPTER FIVE

THE MEANING OF LIFE

*"Go into all the world and preach the gospel
to all creation." (Mark 16:15)*

*"We take it for granted that the object of the Christian ministry is
to convert sinners and to edifying the body of Christ. No faithful
minister can possibly rest short of this. Applause, fame, popularity,
honor, wealth—all these are vain. If souls are not won, if saints
are not matured, our ministry itself is vain." —Horatius Bonar*

PRISON MINISTRY IS one of the greatest evangelistic
ministries on the planet. But I'm somewhat biased
in this regard. After all, where else can you go where
they toss you into a roomful of hardened unbelievers and
then lock the doors so that none can leave until you're
finished sharing the gospel? Yes, I do believe jail ministry
just might be the world's best place for evangelism.

THE PRECIOUS QUALITY OF SAVING FAITH

Being a religious volunteer in the State of California's
penal system, I have the marvelous privilege of speaking

to men from all walks of life about not only how to get saved, but what it means to truly live the Christian life.

Some weeks back I was preaching through Psalm 51 during an evening chapel service to about forty inmates. I was explaining to the men that King David was begging God to do absolutely everything for him. Begging, because he knew that left to himself and his own deficient power, he'd have no hope of ever receiving forgiveness.

In Psalm 51 we find King David calling out to God, saying, "Be gracious to me" (verse 1), "blot out my transgressions" (verse 1), "wash me" (verse 2), "cleanse me" (verse 2), "purify me" (verse 7), "wash me" (verse 7), "make me" (verse 8), "blot out all my iniquities" (verse 9), "create in me" (verse 10), "renew a steadfast spirit within me" (verse 10), "do not cast me away from Your presence" (verse 11), "do not take Your Holy Spirit from me" (verse 11), "restore to me" (verse 12), "sustain me" (verse 12), "deliver me" (verse 14), and "open my lips" (verse 15). It is a psalm commemorating our depraved impotence and the Lord's merciful omnipotence. Pouring himself out to the Lord in repentant song, David confessed his complete inability to put himself in a right relationship with God, apart from the Lord doing absolutely all of it for him.

And that is the beginning of the gospel in a nutshell.

One of the inmates in attendance that evening was a Hispanic gentleman named Juan. At the end of the service, Juan walked up to me, shook my hand, and as tears poured down his face, said, "I want to do what you said. I want to surrender my life to God. I need His forgiveness." I smiled at God's amazing grace. "Then do it," I said. "Repent! Surrender your life to the Savior, trust in the Lord, and give God all the glory." He did, and the Lord mercifully saved Juan's soul that very night.

Since that chapel service in the jail, Juan has written me a few letters. I'd like to share an excerpt from a recent one so that you can relish the greatness of God and the precious quality of saving faith. I would prefer you read it precisely as he wrote it—word for word—questionable grammar and all.

> Hi Charles. Thanx for everything. I really like to hear your message I surrender my life to Jesus christ with your help 8-16 Im walking in faith can you please pray for me. Charles I consider you a friend I would really like to hang out with you when I get out. I really want to change my life and Im starting to now. Thanx Faith Hope love. Love, your friend Juan

Like so many before him, Juan heard the gospel message and surrendered to its demands of repentance toward God and faith in Jesus Christ. The Lord saved him, and now—by God's grace alone—he is a passionate disciple of Jesus Christ, conducting small group Bible studies and prayer groups with the other inmates scattered around his cellblock.

There is so much ministry yet to be done.

YOU ARE TO MAKE DISCIPLES—
NOT CONVERTS

As a genuine believer, when it comes to fulfilling God's will for your life, your role in this world is a lot like mine. And Juan's, too. Our role is to proclaim the biblical gospel of repentance toward God and faith in Jesus Christ to anyone and everyone who will listen. Our objective in life is to both grow in our relationship with God and make others into disciples of Jesus Christ.

In other words, we've been called to live for Christ—not to convert souls!

Did you catch that?

Nothing you or I could ever say or do—apart from the Holy Spirit's regenerating work—will ever cause a person who is dead spiritually to be born again. Sorry to burst your evangelistic bubble, but it's the truth. When it comes to the work of salvation, we can't manufacture it, duplicate it, replicate it, imitate it, conjure it up, or even create a more worshipful atmosphere in order to enhance its probability. We are truly powerless in this regard.

Commenting on this very subject, Pastor Mark Dever wrote, "According to the Bible, converting people is not in our power. And evangelism may not be defined in terms of results but only in terms of faithfulness to the message preached."[65] It's not our responsibility to ultimately ensure that a person's name is written down in the Lamb's Book of Life (though the quality of a person's lifestyle will help us make a reasonable judgment as to whether or not it is). We certainly need to test and examine ourselves to see if we are in the faith, but that's something we assess internally in ourselves—not in others.

To put it another way, we are fruit inspectors—not the Creator of the fruit.

---

65 Mark Dever, The Gospel & Personal Evangelism (Crossway Books, 2007), page 79.

THE BUCK STOPS HERE

You're not responsible for anyone's salvation, much less their eternal condemnation. That verdict is left solely up to God's sovereign mercy and the sinner's own responsibility. It is for this blessed reason that Jesus instructed the local church to make disciples, not to convert souls.

Be sure to grasp this critical point about God's plan for your ministry.

Great Commission Discipleship removes the spotlight from shining upon what we cannot see or perceive (spiritual conversion) and illuminates what we can recognize and assess (external actions pointing toward legitimate discipleship). And that, frankly, is a blessing in itself.

We will never be able to conclusively determine whether or not a person is truly saved, although we can easily determine whether or not the person professing faith is active in intentional discipleship. (If a man professes to be saved, yet makes little effort to love God and know Him more intimately, then the legitimacy of his salvation is shaky at best.) No matter how hard we try, we'll never save a single person. God alone does the saving. Yet the opposite also remains equally true. We'll never assign anyone to Hell due to poorly-executed evangelism. God alone does that, due to the sinner's own unrepentant heart.

Beloved, it is not your responsibility to regenerate the souls of this planet's walking dead.

"We don't fail in our evangelism," wrote Mark Dever, "if we faithfully tell the gospel to someone who is not converted; we fail only if we don't faithfully tell the gospel at all. Evangelism itself isn't converting people; it's telling them that they need to be converted and telling them how they can be."[66]

But please don't make the mistake of assuming that we have no role, whatsoever, in the process of salvation. It is God's very will that you do.

IF I ONLY HAD A HAMMER

In His sovereignty, God established both the end of salvation as well as the means to receiving it. Great Commission Discipleship has its purpose. We are the very means God uses to herald the saving gospel of repentant faith in Jesus Christ alone. Without the cooperation of obedient Christians from around the world, anyone who gets saved would have to be so through miraculous intervention. Sort of like what Jesus did with Saul of Tarsus on the road to Damascus. But divine intervention isn't what Christ had in mind for Great Commission Discipleship. He chose, instead, to use loving laborers like you. You are an instrument of righteousness in the hands of a holy God. A sharpened tool wielded by the compassionate Lord of Heaven and Earth.

You've probably noticed that a hammer is nothing but inanimate steel and wood. In other words, it contains no power to wield itself. Yet when the hammer is swung by the omnipotent arm of the Master Carpenter, it will certainly influence the nail.

I like what author Randy Newman had to say about the matter: "Not only do the minds of nonbelievers need

---

66 Mark Dever, <u>The Gospel & Personal Evangelism</u> (Crossway Books, 2007), page 82.

to be persuaded, but also their knees need to buckle."[67] That's a great picture of Great Commission Discipleship. God persuades the minds of unbelievers, which inevitably results in a lifelong process of knee-buckling discipleship.

Question: Have your knees ever buckled like that?

GOD'S WILL IS FOR YOU TO MAKE DISCIPLES

Jesus taught that His plan of Great Commission Discipleship would be to use clay pots like you and me to make others into radically new creatures. You've been specifically handpicked by the God of this universe to exhort people to commit to Jesus as Master and Lord of their souls.

What a mind-blowing privilege!

What do you think about that? Amazing, right? You are fresh, moldable clay in the hands of the master Potter. He is continuously sculpting you according to His own power, purpose, and plan. He's forming you into a passionate, supernatural disciple-making machine.

Jesus told His disciples, "Follow Me, and *I will make you* fishers of men" (emphasis mine).[68] We do the following—Christ does the making. How wonderfully liberating it is to know that, even though our role in this world is to make others into disciples of Jesus Christ, the Lord really accomplishes the *making* part for us. It is His divine work, after all. The Lord drives the nail of discipleship by wielding the hammer of our obedience. Through our passionate love for

---

67 Randy Newman, <u>Questioning Evangelism</u> (Kregel Publications, 2004), page 35.
68 Matthew 4:19

the souls of men, women, and children, God makes others around our community into disciples of Jesus Christ.

Fishermen study the waters and bait their hooks, but the Lord alone supplies the catch. It has always been this way. There is nothing new under the sun. God is and continues to remain sovereign over all things. It's the same today as it was both on and following the day of Pentecost in Acts chapter two. The early church faithfully went about the business of Great Commission Discipleship—ministering daily in the temple and from house to house—but *"the Lord was adding* to their number day by day those who were being saved" (emphasis mine).[69]

God has always been in the business of building His Church on the shoulders of our obedient love. It is His master plan, after all.

THE PAINS OF APOSTLESHIP

I don't know about you but I am sure glad I wasn't an apostle. After all, as far as we know from Scripture and early Christian writings, all of the apostles were murdered except for the apostle John. And he was sentenced to prison as a wrinkled old man! No, being a legitimate apostle of Jesus Christ was tough, dangerous, painful, and often thankless work.

For instance, consider the apostle Paul when he wrote in 2 Corinthians 11:24–30, admitting this about—not his amazing strength—but his radical *weakness*:

> Five times I received from the Jews thirty-nine lashes. Three times I was beaten with rods, once I

69 Acts 2:47

was stoned, three times I was shipwrecked, a night
and a day I have spent in the deep. I have been on
frequent journeys, in dangers from rivers, dangers
from robbers, dangers from my countrymen, dangers from the Gentiles, dangers in the city, dangers
in the wilderness, dangers on the sea, dangers among
false brethren; I have been in labor and hardship,
through many sleepless nights, in hunger and thirst,
often without food, in cold and exposure. Apart
from such external things, there is the daily pressure
on me of concern for all the churches. Who is weak
without my being weak? Who is led into sin without
my intense concern? If I have to boast, I will boast of
what pertains to my weakness.

Yet that was the kind of passionate disciple-maker God
was looking for to do the miraculous. The weaker the man,
the more the power of God was on display. Once, during
an early missionary journey and immediately after being
stoned and left for dead, Paul got up, marched back into
that crowd of hardened hearts, and "preached the gospel to
that city and had *made many disciples*" (emphasis mine).[70]
When God finds a weak but available hammer, He
reaches for it time and time again.

DISCIPLESHIP REQUIRES CHANGE

Paul understood all about the costs and benefits of having
a deliberate faith. He was both a courageous evangelist and
a compassionate pastor. Upon making those many disciples
in Acts 14:21, he then "returned to Lystra and to Iconium

---

70 Acts 14:21

and to Antioch, strengthening the souls of the disciples, encouraging them to continue in the faith, and saying, 'Through many tribulations we must enter the kingdom of God.' When they had appointed elders for them in every church, having prayed with fasting, they commended them to the Lord in whom they had believed."[71] The apostle Paul was singularly focused on his mission of both making new disciples and edifying the saved disciples, and the Lord was happy to swing that hammer.

Question: What about you? What are you prepared to become (do, start, give up, relocate to, etc.) so that God can use you to win and mature souls? Are you in passionate love with Jesus Christ, or just too busy entertaining the passing pleasures of sin for a season to really care all that much? Is anything in this world more appealing to you than being used by God to manifest His infinite glory? I sure hope not.

The apostle Paul's appointment as an ambassador of Jesus Christ to make disciples of all the nations was not, altogether, unlike ours. Paul made disciples in much the same way we're supposed to, by teaching the Scriptures regularly and sharing our personal testimony with anyone willing to listen. Paul was not ashamed of the gospel, because it is the power of God for salvation to everyone who believes. Although Paul was a unique hammer of uncommon craftsmanship, he was mere flesh and blood like the rest of us.

When the apostle Paul recounted his personal testimony in the presence of King Agrippa, he was careful to

---

71 Acts 14:21-23

mention his purpose in God's ultimate work of salvation, reciting the words of his Lord, who said:

> "But get up and stand on your feet; for this purpose I have appeared to you, to appoint you a minister and a witness not only to the things which you have seen, but also to the things in which I will appear to you; rescuing you from the Jewish people and from the Gentiles, to whom *I am sending you, to open their eyes* so that they may receive forgiveness of sins and an inheritance among those who have been sanctified by faith in Me." (emphasis mine)[72]

As the apostle to the gentiles, Paul was used as a mighty instrument in fulfilling the mission of Great Commission Discipleship—a mission that consisted of being radically used by God to open the blind eyes of those who would receive forgiveness of sins. And you are also a hammer of a similar craftsmanship. You have been commissioned to worship the Lord while making others into disciples of Jesus Christ.

In case you've forgotten, it's the only reason you are still breathing right now. It is God's revealed will for your life today.

THE DIVINE PLAN FOR VICTORY

No one wants to be a loser. Losing is never much fun. The taste of victory has such a flavorful sweetness to it that most athletes practice numerous hours every day preparing for their next competition. No Olympic sprinter,

---

72 Acts 26:16–18

for example, ever runs their race with the goal being to come in second place or—worse yet—finishing dead last.

So when it comes to our own spiritual race of faith, what should we be doing in order to prepare for sure victory over sin and the world?

The mission of the local church is similar to that of an Olympic relay race. It's about running really hard so that you can pass the baton over to the next person, who will then pass the baton over to the next person, who will then pass the baton over to the next person...so that we eventually finish the race and come in first place as a team. The race we run is called *The Glory of God*. Our baton is the *gospel of Jesus Christ*, and the actual passing of the baton is the ministry of *making disciples*. This Christian relay race has quite recently been coined the Great Commission.

GREAT COMMISSION JOB DESCRIPTION

Your church's role in the Great Commission is not about mustering up the sanctified soldiers to *go*. Motivating the saints in your congregation to get up and go is really not the issue at hand regarding Christ's plan for the Great Commission. That's the Holy Spirit's work, not ours. As Christians, our responsibility is to encourage one another toward loving obedience and praying for workers to be scattered throughout the abundant harvest. But the grand work of ultimate motivation rests alone in the hands of the Lord.

Jesus taught this on at least one occasion when He said, "The harvest is plentiful, but the workers are few. Therefore beseech the Lord of the harvest to send out workers into His harvest."[73] From our earthly perspective, the priority of the Great Commission (the baton-exchange of Christianity) is about making disciples of Jesus Christ who will become passionate disciple-makers themselves. Your life's purpose is about disciple-making, not about collecting shiny possessions, getting a better job, or even laying guilt trips before your brothers and sisters in the faith for not sharing their faith as much as maybe you do.

On multiple occasions and over the course of the forty days between His resurrection and ascension, Jesus commissioned the disciples with a clear objective that called for spiritual duplication. To comprehend what Jesus had in mind requires identifying a few key ingredients in the discipleship recipe. One of these ingredients is in understanding the significance of at least one word in the original text of the Bible.

This Greek word is the key to unlocking the knowledge of God's revealed will for living a victorious life.

VERBS, PARTICIPLES, AND IMPERATIVES

The word translated "make disciples" in Matthew 28:19-20, the Great Commission passage, is the Greek word "mathēteuō." Jesus said, "Go therefore and *make disciples* of all the nations, baptizing them in the name of the Father and the Son and the Holy Spirit, teaching them to observe all that I commanded you" (emphasis mine).

You've probably read that famous passage hundreds of times before, automatically placing the emphasis of the

---

73 Matthew 9:37-38

Great Commission on the word "go." After all, it's the first word translated for us in the verse, right? Besides that, most Christians feel like spiritual disasters when they ponder both the inadequacy and irregularity in which they share the gospel with unbelievers. Both assumptions, as you'll now see, are incorrect. Understanding your personal mission in this world requires not a focus on the Greek participle translated "go," but on the verb "mathēteuō," which is translated "make disciples."

In the Greek, "mathēteuō" is the main verb in the sentence. In other words, this little Greek word is the crux of why we are here on Earth right now. The main verb is the main thing. It's why we woke up this morning and why we're still breathing air. The Great Commission is not something you plan to do at a certain time of the day, week, or month; it's something you are doing right now!

As genuine believers, we are currently engaged in the process of making disciples of Jesus Christ, whether we're comfortable doing it or not. The Greek verb's continual present tense implies that we are *already* and *always* active in the process of making disciples and that the job, frankly, will continue until we're no longer alive.

The real issue, then, is not so much, "Now that you're saved, when will you go and make disciples?" but rather, "How effective are you at making disciples now that you're saved?" That is a significant difference. Making disciples is a 24/7 job for a Christian. We are always on the clock. There are no vacations, no holidays, and no sabbaticals. It's something we are required to do for others, and it is something you're always doing for yourself. Remember,

Great Commission Discipleship is the reason you are still breathing right now. It is God's will for your life today.

"Make disciples" (mathēteuō) carries the idea of determined motivation manifested by intense labor. In other words, it requires our full concentration and power. It's non-optional behavior for anyone who names the name of Christ, regardless of whether you are young or old, sick or healthy, a babe in Christ or even a seminary professor with more letters after your name than there are in the alphabet. The ministry of making disciples is the primary objective for local churches, both gathered in fellowship and when scattered throughout the nations.

MORE THAN YOUR G.P.A.

The spiritual lifestyle of a genuine *disciple*, then, as understood from this Greek word (*mathēteuō*), means so much more than a common churchgoer who understands the basic teachings of Christianity. More so than even a churchgoer mainly concerned about checking off duties from a religious to-do list. The root of the word has the idea of a true disciple being someone who persistently believes, with both an internal and external desire to learn more about their subject of interest. For genuine disciples of Christianity, the subject of our passion is Jesus Christ Himself.

The word "disciple" is not a term that could be used, for example, to describe a college student who completes his homework solely because his tuition-paying parents expect it. It would more adequately define a student who personally applies for admission to a specific university due to a heartfelt interest in attending that institution, desires to be instructed by that school's professors in the major he is most interested in, and is willing to get a job in order to pay for it himself, if that's what is required to make it happen.

Question: Which definition of "student" best describes you when it comes to loving and learning about the Lord Jesus Christ? Is it more of a *have to* item for you, or a *get to* blessing? Are you loving and learning more about Jesus every day, or merely going through the religious motions of a convenient Christianity? Are you being conformed to the image of Jesus Christ, or just checking God off your weekly to-do list?

If you are not obeying the first prerequisite of God's revealed will, what makes you think God would ever disclose His will in other areas of your life?

BACKED INTO AN UNCOMFORTABLE CORNER

A jailed inmate walked up to me after a chapel service one Saturday afternoon. He said, "I need you to tell me what God wants me to do."

"Sure," I replied, "what's the problem?"

"My lawyer says that if I lie about where I was during the fight, then I'll be set free. But if I tell the truth, then I'm looking at five to ten years. What should I do?"

I've been cornered by inmates many times with similar questions, and by that time I knew how to handle it. Typically, questions like this are best answered by answering nothing at all. In fact, Jesus used this strategy on multiple occasions Himself. The best way to deal with it is to have the person answer the question for him- or herself.

I then responded, "Before I give you my opinion, answer a question first for me. Do you think God would rather have you tell the truth in court or be found a liar?"

"God probably wants me to tell the truth, but then I'd be stuck—"

"I'm ready to give you my answer now," I interrupted. "I agree with you. I think you're right in that God would rather have you tell the truth—even if it means going to jail—rather than being found a liar."

He knew it was the correct answer. I never saw him again after that. He wasn't truly searching for God's will in his life. He just wanted an excuse. A way out of his self-inflicted predicament.

SPIRITUAL SLACKERS NEED NOT APPLY

In describing the noun form of this particular Greek word (*mathēteuō*), W. E. Vine's *Expository Dictionary of New Testament Words* says, "A disciple was not only a pupil, but an adherent; hence they are spoken of as imitators of their teacher."[74] In other words, there is no room in the Greek word translated "make disciples" for spiritual slackers who manifest no desire to learn, imitate, or grow in the knowledge of Christ! This definition of a genuinely saved disciple could hardly be used to describe the average American churchgoer who attends church for seventy-five minutes on Sunday mornings, yet commits to little or no spiritual disciplines during the rest of the week.

---

74 W.E. Vine, Expository Dictionary of New Testament Words (Fleming H. Revell Company, 1966), page 316.

Jesus put it this way, "A pupil is not above his teacher; but everyone, after he has been fully trained, will be like his teacher."[75]

My wife, for example, would know something was terribly wrong with our marriage if I only came home for a couple hours, once or twice every seven days. She'd have good reason to question the level of my love and commitment, both to her and to our marriage.

The same goes for your relationship with God. He wants every part of you or absolutely nothing from you. God is a jealous God that way.

ONLY THE PLAYERS GET TO PLAY

I love watching football. A few years ago the Green Bay Packers won the Superbowl and—since I'm from Wisconsin—that made me a happy fan. Like most Packer fans from that great state, I have Green Bay Packer paraphernalia scattered around my house (a Packer shirt, a Packer cheese hat, Green Bay Packer slippers, a Packer blanket, etc.). I even had the privilege of attending a Green Bay Packer playoff game once at Lambeau Field.

During that game, my friends and I wore Green Bay Packer jerseys (just like the real players), and we cheered for the team in much the same way the actual players cheered on their own teammates. We were all in the same stadium, rooting for the same team, and wearing the same uniforms. Yet no matter how much I wanted to, they wouldn't let me go onto the field to hike the ball or throw a pass. In fact, they'd have arrested me had I tried. The coach

---

75 Luke 6:40

didn't know my name, and the front office never paid me a dime to show up for the game. I associated myself with the Packers, cheered for them, wore their colors, and followed them throughout the year, but I was never really on the team. It turns out that there's a considerable difference between being a paid professional football player and being an obnoxious fan. The main difference, apparently, is having a signed contract. A contract which I, like so many others who showed up at Lambeau Field that day, lacked.

NOBODY LIKES A POSER

Pseudo-Christians are a lot like spiritual posers. They arrive at the stadium (church) on game day (Sunday), put on their team's jersey (carry a Bible), and hang out with the real players (God's children), but the fact is, they're not on the team's roster (Lamb's Book of Life). They are not genuine Christians. They look a lot alike from a distance, but they don't have a signed contract with the upper management. When they die and stand before the Owner of this universe, they'll profess to have performed some amazing feats. Unfortunately, Christ will respond to their baseless assertions with little more than, "I never knew you, DEPART FROM ME, YOU WHO PRACTICE LAWLESSNESS."[76]

Author Francis Chan wrote, "Lukewarm people say they love Jesus, and he is, indeed, a part of their lives. But only a part. They give him a section of their time, their money, and their thoughts, but he isn't allowed to control their lives."[77] That certainly is not the sort of person Jesus

---

76 Matthew 7:23
77 Francis Chan, <u>Crazy Love</u> (David C. Cook, 2008), page 72.

had in mind when He used the Greek word *mathēteuō*, translated "make disciples." Legitimate disciples of Jesus Christ are deliberate and radical about their faith. They are never lukewarm.

Frankly, when I learned what the Bible actually teaches about what it truly means to make disciples of Jesus Christ, the Great Commission mandate of intentional discipleship leapt from the pages of my Bible. I finally began to more clearly understand God's revealed will for both my life and my ministry. This was a tremendous blessing because it also removed the throbbing guilt of my own evangelistic inadequacies. It provided me with a greater appreciation for the Master's plan of Great Commission Discipleship and, particularly, my function in it.

My prayer is that it would for you, too.

How to Talk to Sinners

During His earthly ministry, Jesus confronted the depraved sinners of this world in a variety of ways. Sometimes we see the Lord discipling a few men in a garden late in the evening, while at other times He was preaching passionately in the open air to thousands along the seashore. Once we find Him reclining at the home of a tax collector— surrounded by party mongers, drunkards, and harlots— yet even then He was teaching sinners the good news.

Our Lord was in the world, but He was never influenced by the world. He was a friend to sinners, yet experienced no fellowship with wicked acquaintances.

He spoke to an adulterous Samaritan woman next to a well, to a demon-possessed man who came running out of the tombs, and He even rebuked the elite Pharisees of His day for their hypocritical ritualism. Jesus taught in the temple while but a youth of twelve years, conversed with disciples of the locust-eating baptizer, and even relinquished morsels of glory in the presence of the high priest after being handcuffed in Gethsemane's garden.

Yet still He spoke the everlasting gospel.

He fed the five thousand in the wilderness, raised a stinking Lazarus from the dead, sat alone and hungry in the wilderness for forty days being tempted by Satan, and quoted Scripture as He hung on the timbers of Calvary. In every circumstance of life, we see the Lord resting upon the Scriptures, instructing multitudes, discipling those in His inner circle, offering words of eternal assurance to a redeemed thief hanging next to Him on a cross, and otherwise performing the will of His Father.

Jesus Christ is the true pattern for Great Commission Discipleship which every one of us must strive to imitate today.

In the Great Commission passages of Matthew, Mark, Luke, John, and Acts, we see many important features of Christian living to be aware of. We see Christ's authority for sending us out into the world,[78] we learn the message He gave us to teach,[79] we're told where to go and whom to speak to,[80] He tells us He will be with us as we go,[81] we're given instructions about what to do with those people who believe our message,[82] and we're even told that we'll be

---

78 c.f. Matthew 28:18 and John 20:21
79 c.f. Luke 24:47 and Mark 16:15
80 c.f. Acts 1:8 and Mark 16:20
81 c.f. Matthew 28:20 and Mark 16:20
82 c.f. Matthew 28:19-20

supremely gifted in the work.[83] What I find so intriguing, however, is that the one critical element altogether absent is anything having to do with the *method* (or means) in which we're to specifically fulfill this Great Commission.

Behold the wisdom of the God we serve!

THE CHOICE OF MINISTRY IS ALL YOURS

What I mean by this is that the very choice of ministry is left to your own personal discretion, based upon both the desires of your heart and your God-given spiritual giftedness. Not many of us are called to stand on a soapbox and preach into the open air, but you're free to do so if you've got the nerve. We are not commanded to specifically hand out gospel tracts at bus stops, but you're given that liberty if such a ministry is placed on your heart. We are not instructed in the Great Commission passages to visit hospitals, go to prisons, fly overseas to build church facilities for missionaries, visit the homes of people who visit our churches, or even to conduct activities such as Vacation Bible School, faith-based homeless shelters, or neighborhood swimming pool parties for single mothers and their children. Yet you're free to make disciples along such avenues if you have the inclination to do so.

Every genuine Christian is radically endowed with spectacular speaking and/or serving gifts, and no two believers are exactly alike. You are as unique as a snowflake that falls from the heavens. God supernaturally gifted you for ministry in a way that He has never gifted anyone since.

---

83 c.f. Luke 24:45 and Acts 1:9

What a marvelous truth to consider.

Other believers might possess the gift of speaking while you may be supremely gifted with the tools of mercy or administration. A woman might have the spiritual gift of encouragement while her husband is sovereignly equipped with the gift of helps. Christians are free to minister to children, teenagers, adults, the elderly, to foreigners in third-world countries, or in any other mixture of the world's demographics—both in Christian and non-Christian circles alike. We are individual members in the Body of Christ, and we've been equipped to minister to one another—and the world at large—through the gifts given to us at the moment of our rebirth. The means in which you minister along the canvas of God's Great Commission plan are left up to your own personal choice.

How awesome is that?

J.I. Packer wrote:

> Such was evangelism according to Paul: going out in love, as Christ's agent in the world, to teach sinners the truth of the Gospel with a view to converting and saving them. If, therefore, we are engaging in this activity, in this spirit, and with this aim, we are evangelizing, irrespective of the particular means by which we are doing it.[84]

But please notice that this sovereign *omission* in our Lord's Great Commission leaves every one of us without excuse for not being intentional about our own progressive

---

84 J.I. Packer, <u>Evangelism & the Sovereignty of God</u> (InterVarsity Press, 1961), page 53.

sanctification. There is no legitimate excuse you or I could ever claim for not being proactive in some kind of ministry to someone in need. If you're alive and conscious, then your age, theological training, and physical health are all equally irrelevant. God wants to use you in ministry. His desire is to swing that hammer! If the Lord of glory was finished with you, then you'd be up in Heaven rather than here right now.

FOR MORE THAN JUST PASTORS

A friend of mine recently told me about a 104-year-old woman who regularly shared the gospel with the community of people at the assisted living facility where she lived. You may be an elderly, silver-haired saint less than a breath away from glory, but you're not in Heaven yet. Fulfill your mission. Fulfill God's revealed will for your life today!

If the Lord had said that the only means for accomplishing Great Commission Discipleship was for pastors to preach from the pulpit on Sunday mornings, then the rest of the congregation would have a watertight excuse for not being directly involved in making disciples. However, because Jesus didn't give any such instruction, you're free to brainstorm how you might best be used to manifest God's glory to all the nations.

J.I. Packer further concluded, "The principle is that the best method of evangelism is the one which serves the gospel most completely.... What that best method is in each case, you and I have to find out for ourselves. It is in light of this principle that all debates about evangelistic methods must be decided."[85]

So choose a ministry and busy yourself with serving others in that ministry. That is God's revealed will for your life today.

PASSIONATE DISCIPLESHIP NEVER ENDS

It's been some two thousand years since our sovereign Lord ascended into the clouds, yet He remains eternally the same yesterday and today and forever. Jesus had the wisdom and foresight to gaze into the generations ahead and behold the meandering road which His followers would travel down throughout the centuries. It was with such omniscience that He prayed to the Father, "I do not ask on behalf of these alone, but for those who believe in Me *through their word*" (emphasis mine).[86] Jesus knew that the ministries of local evangelism, foreign missions, and overall discipleship would be a lifelong work of continual progress.

It will go on and on, until the tares are finally separated from the wheat.

There was one Person who lived perfectly in this world, and it wasn't you or me. Therefore, we're all capable of learning more and growing more in our love for Jesus Christ. The most spiritually-minded, biblically astute person can always increase in both knowledge and application. We will never achieve a state of sinless perfection in this life. Thus, we should each confess our sins, repent daily, pray for the Lord's forgiveness, and begin afresh

85 *Ibid,* (InterVarsity Press, 1961), page 91.
86 John 17:20

each morning with the goal of being a more passionate disciple of Jesus Christ.

We are to never cease teaching others all that Jesus commanded, as well as the other God-breathed truths contained in Holy Scripture. We're to strive toward living out the faith that is in us. One important feature of obedient Christian living that you must never lose sight of is the fact that you are also to be discipled, not merely disciple others.

Did you catch that?

Yes, you need to be mentored by mature saints and not merely mentor other people.

ONCE SAVED, ALWAYS SANCTIFYING

As mentioned earlier, Great Commission Discipleship is as much about your own progressive sanctification as it is about other people's salvation. The Great Commission is as much about your own maturing relationship with Jesus Christ as it is about other people getting saved.

Every Paul needs a Timothy to mentor, and every Timothy needs a Paul to be molded by. Great Commission Discipleship is something we fulfill both directly and indirectly. We are *directly* fulfilling God's plan of Great Commission Discipleship when we're personally making others into disciples of Jesus Christ. But we're also *indirectly* accomplishing His will when we're being taught and discipled by other believers.

Just because God saved you doesn't mean the Great Commission ceased for you from that moment forward. Remember, the mission of the church is to "Go therefore and make disciples of all the nations, baptizing them in the name of the Father and the Son and the Holy Spirit, *teaching them to observe all* that I commanded you" (emphasis mine).[87] Learning persistent obedience to the will of God is just as important as your regeneration is. When God saved you, at that very moment, you began a lifelong process of obedience to all the things you're being taught from the Scriptures. The mandate of Great Commission Discipleship continues on and on, even till your dying breath.

No Christian is ever exempt from Christ's discipleship model, either. Neither age, gender, race, geography, culture, nor even spiritual maturity removes us from the discipleship process.

So press on, dear Christian, being diligent to work out your own "salvation with fear and trembling; for it is God who is at work in you, both to will and to work for His good pleasure."[88]

---

87 Matthew 28:19–20
88 Philippians 2:12–13

CHAPTER SIX

WHAT DO YOU DO AT A GREEN LIGHT?

"A wide door for effective service has opened to me, and there are many adversaries." (1 Corinthians 16:9)

"Men often tell me they don't know how to share their faith, or they don't think they know enough Bible or theology to be able to share their faith. For these reasons, they shy away from opportunities that might arise for reaching others for Christ." —Jim George

THE MOST IMPATIENT person on the planet is the guy waiting in the second car at a red stoplight, three seconds after it turns green.

A series of events usually occurs in those craziest of moments. Usually the guy waiting starts talking to himself, saying things like, "Come on, buddy!" A split second later, he smacks both hands on the car horn as if ordaining it for vehicular ministry.

Startled, the perpetrator in the first car jerks awake from

his daydream, wondering what all the excitement is about. He glances up, sees the dazzling green lights staring back at him, and then hastily slams his foot on the gas, all the while checking his rearview mirror to see just how annoyed the guy behind him really is. He stays ahead of every car behind him, because the last thing he wants to do is have to look over and mouth the expected apology.

Sound familiar? I'm sad to admit it, but there have been times in my own life when I've found myself sitting in the driver's seat of both those cars. Shame on me. And yet, I can also see myself driving both of those cars from a spiritual perspective as well.

Do you know what I mean?

Occasionally, I find myself sitting in the second car, frustrated and honking my spiritual horn because life is not going like I hoped it would. Yet at other times I know I've also been the slacker daydreaming in the first car while other people—and particularly the Lord—are honking their horns at me, trying to motivate me to get a move on and burn some ministry-rubber.

Have you ever felt like you have been sitting in one of those two spiritual cars? Yes, I think we all have.

So the question you need to answer when trying to determine God's unrevealed will for your life, then, is this: *When the Lord gives me the green light for ministry, what should I do?*

WAS JESUS INTO ISSUING RECOMMENDATIONS?

On the day of Pentecost in Acts chapter two, the apostle Peter didn't hesitate to preach through the open air to the thousands of Jews who were amazed at the outpouring of the Holy Spirit. He simply responded with his spiritual gift and ministered in a way that glorified the Lord. God responded to Peter's radical obedience to the commands of Great Commission Discipleship by saving 3,000 souls from the eternal lake of fire.

When the Lord commanded Phillip to go and witness to the Ethiopian eunuch out in the middle of a desert, he didn't waste precious moments vacillating about what to say once he overtook the chariot.[89] Phillip simply did as he was told. He didn't fret over how best to start a religious conversation with the high-ranking foreigner, nor even how he would make the transition from the natural realm to the spiritual. He simply went. And through Phillip's radical obedience to the commands of Great Commission Discipleship, the Lord responded by saving that eunuch's soul from the wrath to come.

When the apostle Paul journeyed from city to city preaching the gospel to both Jews and Gentiles alike, he knew it would be difficult work. Countless more people rejected his message than believed it. In fact, he ministered with the Lord's assurance that much more than mere rejection awaited him in every city he entered.

Luke recorded Paul's words in Acts 20:22-23 when he confessed: "And now, behold, bound by the Spirit, I am on

---

89 See Acts 8:26-39

my way to Jerusalem, not knowing what will happen to me there, except that the Holy Spirit solemnly testifies to me in every city, saying that bonds and afflictions await me."

Yet despite that perplexing reality hanging over his head, Paul remained passionate about fulfilling his assigned ministry. He responded by saying, "But I do not consider my life of any account as dear to myself, so that I may finish my course and the ministry which I received from the Lord Jesus, to testify solemnly of the gospel of the grace of God."[90]

Paul was sold out to the demands of Great Commission Discipleship, and the Lord worked through him mightily because of it.

WHAT TO EXPECT TODAY

Modern-day Christians should expect similar results when sharing the gospel with boldness, joy, and compassionate love. We can expect heaping spoonfuls of both acceptance and rejection, and in varying measures as well.

Jesus forewarned His disciples (the application remains true for many Christians today as well) that sinners "will lay their hands on you and will persecute you, delivering you to the synagogues and prisons, bringing you before kings and governors for My name's sake. It will lead to an opportunity for your testimony."[91] Yet the Lord also offered encouragement for our loyalty as well, concluding that divine lesson by saying, "By your endurance you will gain your lives."[92]

---

90 Acts 20:24
91 Luke 21:12-13
92 Luke 21:19

We are rarely more Christ-like than when we are graciously sharing the good news with sinners who outright reject the message and persecute us. Though rejection and maltreatment are neither our aim nor even a prayerful outcome of Great Commission Discipleship, it is, nevertheless, a normal byproduct of sharing the gospel with both sin-loving God-haters and—sadly—nominal churchgoers.

COFFEE SHOP EVANGELISM

With that said, however, you're probably a lot like most American Christians in that you're yet to have anyone cast stones at you as happened to Stephen. Or have certain Jews from Antioch and Iconium travel all the way to Lystra just to stone you like they did with Paul in Acts chapter fourteen.

In our contemporary western culture, it's practically unheard of to be physically assaulted just because you shared the good news of repentant faith with a sinner. I am not saying that it never happens in our "civilized" culture, because it certainly does on occasion. All I am saying is that it's a rare moment when a Christian gets punched in the face because they did little more than share with someone in a coffee shop about how to get to Heaven.

Not all cultures are like ours, unfortunately. (Or rather, fortunately?)

NO ONE SAID THIS WOULD BE EASY

Many churches across America financially support missionaries in hostile cultures where we cannot publicly advertise their names or the countries they minister in for fear of their exile and/or bodily injury. Yet with the many possible outcomes of sharing our most precious faith, Jesus offered words of immense encouragement when He said, "Blessed are you when people insult you and persecute you, and falsely say all kinds of evil against you because of me. Rejoice and be glad, for your reward in heaven is great; for in the same way they persecuted the prophets who were before you."[93]

Despite the seemingly negative results that may accompany obedience to the gospel, however, the contemporary Church needs to remain focused regarding its core business to go and make disciples. Ultimately, we need to be more concerned about other people's souls than we are about protecting our own necks.

It's hard to do, I know. Jesus never said it would be easy. If it was easy, then everyone would already be doing it.

When Jesus issued the Great Commission to go out into all the nations and preach the gospel, He wasn't offering a sanctified suggestion or even a take-it-or-leave-it recommendation to the Church at large. It wasn't a parable with a hidden meaning, and it certainly was not meant to be an obscure speech set aside for the super-saints who sell everything and move to the jungles of Africa, either.

The mandate of Great Commission Discipleship is as valid for each of us today as it was for the early disciples who fixed their gaze on the clouds as Jesus ascended into glory.

DEAD MEN TELL NO TALES

Immediately after declaring His deity and the extent of His authoritative position throughout the universe, Jesus issued some radical instructions to the local church, the

---

93 Matthew 5:11-12

first of which is that we must go. He told His disciples, "Go therefore and make disciples of all the nations."[94]

Great Commission Discipleship does not sit still. Obeying God's revealed will requires us engaging in holy activity. To "go" suggests movement. It requires leaving the comforts of A in order to get to B. Great Commission Discipleship requires departing from the convenience of where we are at currently and going to where we are most needed. It is impossible to go if we refuse to budge. Or to say it more biblically, if you are not *going* then you are not breathing. Holy discipleship is always on the move. Passion for the things of God inevitably results in sacred movement for the glory of Christ.

THE MOST FEARED WORD IN CHRISTENDOM

The Greek word in the Matthew 28:19 text translated "go" is not an overly remarkable word. You don't need a master's degree in theology to grasp the fullness of its meaning. It simply means *go*. Nothing special, just *go*. Yet just because the word is uncomplicated and rather easy to understand linguistically doesn't mean there is nothing more to be learned from it.

The Greek word translated "go" is a supporting participle with a direct relationship to the imperative verb ("make disciples"), which makes it also an imperative. In other words, because the verb translated "make disciples" is the main command in the sentence and is in the imperative mood, all the words linked to or closely associated with it also take on its mood. For all of us grammar flunkies, a word in the imperative mood means that it is a command.

---

94 Matthew 28:19

It requires and expects action. It demands obedience. It *must* be done!

This is significant because it teaches us that the crux of Great Commission Discipleship hinges on the verb translated "make disciples," and that the supporting participles ("go," "baptize," and "teach") are simply springboards that describe the actual process of Great Commission Discipleship. Moreover, it drives home the point that there can be no making of Christ-like disciples unless there is first some going on our part. In other words, Christ's plan for biblical discipleship—the purpose of which is to make disciples of the Lord Jesus Christ—finds its very roots in your obedience to *go*.

Even though we all fail miserably from time to time, true disciples of Christ do desire to live godly lives for the glory of God. The apostle Paul wrote that, "*all* who desire to live godly in Christ Jesus *will be persecuted*" (emphasis mine).[95] Persecution, then, tends to be the natural outcome of living a deliberate life of godliness.

And so, if you have never been persecuted for your faith in Jesus Christ, what might that be saying about your current level of godliness?

A SPIRITUAL CHECK UP

Have you ever been persecuted for living godly in the midst of those around you? You've probably never been physically assaulted, but has anyone ever laughed at your desire to live for Christ and make His name well known?

---

95 2 Timothy 3:12

If not, that might be an indication that something isn't quite right with your soul.

Don't get me wrong. I'm not saying that you are definitely not a true believer if you're not on fire for God. What I am suggesting, however, is that maybe you should do what the apostle Paul said and, "Test yourself to see if you are in the faith; examine yourselves!"[96]

THE DIVINE APPOINTMENT SETTER

Recently I went to the mall to hand out gospel tracts and talk to people about Jesus. Toward the end of that evening, a college student came up to me with shopping bags clutched in each of his hands. His five friends stood off to the side—confused—wondering what in the world he was doing. The young man then said to me, "I don't know who you are or what you're handing out, but I feel that I need to take whatever it is you're giving away."

God is so good to set up divine appointments like that. I talked with that young man for about ten minutes while his friends just stared at us. He confessed to me that he grew up in the church and came from a good family, but that he wasn't walking with God. Not even close. He admitted that if he died that night, he wasn't exactly sure where he would end up. We talked more about the gospel, and I gave him some Christian literature from our church.

I then exhorted him to get right with God before it's too late, because no one is guaranteed tomorrow. Including him.

---

96 2 Corinthians 13:5

THE GREAT OMISSION

If Christians refuse to *go*, then—humanly speaking—disciples of Jesus Christ will not be made. Paul explained it this way when he wrote, "How will they call on Him in whom they have not believed? How will they believe in Him whom they have not heard? And how will they hear without a preacher? How will they preach unless they are sent? Just as it is written, 'HOW BEAUTIFUL ARE THE FEET OF THOSE WHO BRING GOOD NEWS OF GOOD THINGS!'"[97] God is sovereign over all things—to be sure—yet He has purposefully designed the plan of Great Commission Discipleship to be in accordance with our obedience to go.

This is truly significant because Jesus was saying that *going* is non-optional behavior for a believer. Remember, you are a hammer that Christ wants to wield. God will swing the hammer of salvation. Great Commission Discipleship is imperative. Evangelism and sanctification are commanded. Disobedience is unacceptable behavior. The contemporary Church may have allowed the Great Commission to regress into the Great *Omission*, but it's certainly no mere suggestion. It is the glorious mission we are set apart for in this godless world. We need to be passionate, deliberate, and persistent about it.

Christians are the brass and strings in the divine orchestra, but the Lord alone conducts the symphony of salvation. Don't ever forget that.

We must become enamored with God's crazy love, both for saving sinners and edifying the saints. Frankly,

---

97 Romans 10:14–15

you and I haven't been offered a choice in the matter. Great Commission Discipleship is to be both a liberating and joy-producing privilege, never a bothersome chore. It also just so happens to be the main function of God's revealed plan for your life today.

YOU ARE NOT A DIPLOMAT

As a genuine lover of God, you're a living witness to the gospel of Jesus Christ. Whether you are comfortable with that reality or not, you're a living 24/7 witness for Jesus Christ. In a deeper sense, then, every Christian is a witness to the gospel regardless of his or her own level of faithfulness to the King. So the real issue is not "Get up and get going," but rather, "How effective are you at being a witness for Jesus Christ now that you're saved and commissioned?"

This is quite true and more mind-boggling than you might imagine.

A diplomat is someone who represents a single, self-regulating government and conducts relations with the governments of foreign nations. The diplomat's function, essentially, is to do whatever he or she can in order to make foreign nations feel comfortable about doing business with the diplomat's own government. They are wine-and-dine types who try to get others around them to feel relaxed and more at ease.

One author humorously commented that a diplomat is "a person who can tell you to go to hell in such a way that you actually look forward to the trip."[98] Although comical,

---

98 QuoteGarden.com, Caskie Stinett, Out of the Red, www.quotegarden.com/ diplomacy.html (accessed January 4, 2013).

that certainly doesn't describe a Christian's function here in this world. Not hardly. Christians are not spiritual diplomats trying to relate to the tares and other sinners of this age. We're not trying to be buddies with sinners, and our chief business is not getting sinners to relate better to us, either.

We are ambassadors for Jesus Christ, not wine-and-dine diplomats.

YOU ARE AN AMBASSADOR

In contrast to a diplomat, an ambassador is the highest-ranking representative appointed by a government to represent its own interests, ideals, and opinions to other foreign governments. That is quite different from being a schmoozing diplomat.

Someone who is an *ambassador-at-large* may represent his or her own government to any foreign government around the globe. An *ambassador-extraordinary*, on the other hand, is someone who has been appointed to a specific mission to one government in particular. That's what genuine Christians really are. You are an ambassador on an extraordinary mission to the people of whichever nation you find yourself in at the moment.

As a believer, your role in this fallen world is to passionately represent the God who saved you by making Him well known to everyone outside His kingdom. The apostle Peter wrote, "But you are a chosen race, a royal priesthood, a holy nation, a people for God's own possession, *so that you may proclaim the excellencies of Him who has called you* out of darkness into His marvelous light; for you once were not a people, but now you are the people of God; you had not received mercy, but now you have received mercy" (emphasis mine).[99]

How've you been doing with your ministry of representing God as an ambassador-extraordinary? It is a 24/7 job. We are to be busy with the work both in season and out of season. J.I. Packer wrote, "Every Christian, therefore, has a God-given obligation to make known the gospel of Christ. And every Christian who declares the gospel message to any fellow man does so as Christ's ambassador and representative, according to the terms of his God-given commission."[100]

A Full-Time Job with Benefits

Some ambassadors have been assigned a mission that is dangerous and potentially lethal, aimed at a foreign nation rather hostile to our own government. Others have been assigned to a people group that, while they may enjoy the ambassador's company, is unwilling to defect and become co-citizens with us. Yet every ambassador spends the majority of his or her time outside the country of his or her own citizenship.

Christian ambassadors have a full-time job called Great Commission Discipleship. It's a job we are always a part of, yet many of us aren't very effective while doing it.

Why is that?

Some of us are more asleep on the job than we are at being active in our ambassadorial duties. That's a serious problem, because foreign governments (like most non-Christians you

99 1 Peter 2:9-10
100 J.I. Packer, <u>Evangelism & the Sovereignty of God</u> (InterVarsity Press, 1961), page 46.

know) aren't interested in receiving thousands of ambassadors from other countries. As far as they are concerned, one or two is more than enough.

Genuine Christians long to be with their Abba King. We're drawn nearer to Him each day while being conformed to the image of His Son. Yet until our work here is done, our light is extinguished or the last trumpet sounds, we must be diligent about the business of representing our God's morals, ideals, directions, laws, covenants, judgments, commandments and promises to a people who reject both Him and the message we bring.

Christian disciples proclaim the gospel with authoritative power because "we are ambassadors for Christ, as though God were making an appeal through us."[101] We're to mimic the apostle Paul's desire, "that utterance may be given to me in the opening of my mouth, to make known with boldness the mystery of the gospel, for which I am an ambassador in chains; that in proclaiming it *I may speak boldly, as I ought to speak*" (emphasis mine).[102]

ARE YOU A SPIRITUAL SPY?

An ambassador who refuses to represent the government he's been commissioned by and, instead, conforms himself to the will of a foreign dictator, would at best be considered reckless. It is more likely, however, that such an ambassador would be immediately recalled and subsequently imprisoned for being a spy, if not shot by a firing squad.

Ambassadors receive their marching orders from the government of their citizenship. And for Christians, the

101 2 Corinthians 5:20
102 Ephesians 6:18–20

God of the universe governs our actions. The message He has commissioned us with is called the gospel, and it is a ministry that demands the reconciliation of every creature.

As an ambassador for Christ, your message is crystal clear. Your message to the nations of this world is that our King is coming to war against them and that He'll utterly destroy them unless they wave the white flag of unconditional surrender. Ambassadors go to their assigned country not to make friends, but to speak the truth in love. Fervent, Christ-worshiping, holy love. Christians are to go and teach and plead with sinners to lay down their arms and submit to our Leader, who is truly the King of kings.

Scripture calls this mission of ours a "ministry of reconciliation."

A CHINESE MISSIONARY TO THE U.S.A.

Consider for a moment a young Chinese man who, for most of his life, worshipped as a Buddhist.

Through one way or another, he heard the gospel of Jesus Christ, turned from serving false idols to the living God, and surrendered his soul to Jesus Christ. Over the course of the next few years, he obtained a Bible and began reading the Great Commission passages. Through this study, he became burdened for missions work around the globe. The young Chinese man began praying to God about missionary work and subsequently felt called to leave his Chinese homeland in order to share the good news with people in other nations.

But where should he go?

He grabbed a world map and quickly noticed that the

United States of America was a long way away. He knew those Americans need to hear about Jesus just as much as the Chinese people do. And God called him to go to all the nations, after all. He prayed about it some more and ultimately concluded that God would, indeed, have him serve as a missionary to the natives of California. After doing some more research about the pagan, idolatrous people of California, he decided that the city of Fresno was where he would minister for the rest of his life. He sold all of his possessions and, with little more than a Bible in hand, headed out west to learn a new language and share his faith. He became a foreign missionary to the sinners of Fresno, California.

Sound a bit farfetched? Why is that?

Are the people of Fresno, California, or Appleton, Wisconsin, or Joliet, Illinois, or New York, New York, or Las Vegas, Nevada, or Louisville, Kentucky, or Hell, Michigan (yes, there is a city in Michigan named *Hell*) too *good* for the gospel? Are we so naïve as to believe we don't need as many people as possible sharing the good news of Jesus Christ with those in our own neighborhoods? What a blessing for us that we're already here in the good 'ole U.S.A. We don't even need to travel halfway around the world to another Gentile nation filled with sinners who need to hear the gospel.

How fortunate we all are to be here already.

AMAZING GRACE

Your message to all people everywhere—including your very own city—is both straightforward and compassionate:

We "beg you on behalf of Christ, be reconciled to God."[103] It's a message that every one of us feels uncomfortable sharing at times, but it isn't a difficult message to explain.

We are to exhort sinners to repent of their sin, to be born again, and to surrender to God by faith alone in the Lord Jesus Christ. Why should we be pleading with sinners this way? Because God is in the business of making dead creatures alive and old things new! What a marvelous gospel for people to hear.

Both our mission and our message is "from God, who reconciled us to Himself through Christ and *gave us the ministry of reconciliation*, namely, that God was in Christ reconciling the world to Himself, not counting their trespasses against them, and *He has committed to us* the word of reconciliation" (emphasis mine).[104]

In his book *Living the Cross Centered Life*, C.J. Mahaney wrote:

> What amazing grace! There simply isn't greater news we could give to anyone, anywhere, at any time. And you and I indeed have the privilege as well as the responsibility of proclaiming this good news. We've been entrusted with this unique message about this unique Mediator, and we're the sole guardians of it. That's why we must deeply understand it ourselves and take it to heart, so we can share it accurately and passionately with others.[105]

---

103 2 Corinthians 5:20
104 2 Corinthians 5:18-19
105 C.J. Mahaney, <u>Living the Cross Centered Life</u> (Multnomah Books, 2006), page 73 and 74.

As Christ's ambassadors to all the nations (including this American nation), we're not to be telling sinners that if they'd just throw God a bone and give Him a try, then He would, in return, give them money, possessions, more lands, or even lasting happiness. No, our message is that unless they turn from their sin and place their faith in Jesus Christ alone, our King will grind them to pieces in the winepress of His eternal wrath.

It's called the gospel. It is very, very good news. And it is far and away the most loving message you could ever tell anyone in the world.

Question: Who do you know that needs to hear this message?

ETERNAL RESULTS COME FROM TEMPORARY ACTION

In Acts chapter two and following, the repentant body of believers walked worthy of their high calling. They "continually devoted themselves to the apostles' teaching and to fellowship, to the breaking of bread and to prayer."[106] Yet such devotion was not the extent of their Christian worship. There was more substance to their faith than mere Bible studies and singing hymns of praise. We are told that they were "Day by day continuing with one mind in the temple, and breaking bread from house to house."[107] Their likeminded fellowship was sweet and their passionate love for the risen Messiah emboldened them to meet, greet,

---

106 Acts 2:42
107 Acts 2:46

120

and have spiritual conversations with those in the temple day-by-day.

This one-to-one witnessing was such a potent testimony to the power of the gospel that even the high priest himself complained, "We gave you strict orders not to continue teaching in this name, and yet, you have filled Jerusalem with your teaching."[108]

Later on, we're told that "even a great many of the priests were becoming obedient to the faith."[109] Those priests of Judaism would have been the lower level, bottom-rung priests who ministered in the temple on a daily basis and, therefore, were eyewitnesses to the apostles' public teaching. Yet it's quite logical to conclude these priests also had numerous encounters with the many thousands of non-apostolic Christians and, as a result, saw the radical out-working of the truth that was present in them day-by-day.

Their personal work of Great Commission Discipleship was so potent that the temple ministers of Judaism abandoned the self-righteousness of rituals and ceremonies and submitted to the lordship of Jesus Christ alone. Those priests forsook the man-centered teachings of the scribes, Pharisees, and Sadducees and—like the other believers there in Jerusalem—devoted themselves to the apostolic teachings of fishermen, ex-tax collectors, and the like. Men who possessed the gospel truth.

Those deliberate disciples of the resurrected Messiah walked worthy of the faith that was in them day-by-day. The end result was that God saved even a great many of the priests from the outstretched arms of Hell. A few

---

108 Acts 5:28
109 Acts 6:7

days of joyful labor for an eternity of rewards: that's what Great Commission Discipleship is all about.

Imagine what incredible things the Lord would do through you if you went out day-by-day and purposely proclaimed the only message that is the power of God for salvation to everyone who believes.

Just imagine.

CHAPTER SEVEN

Don't Count Your Tares Before They Hatch

"Or do you not know that the unrighteous will not inherit the kingdom of God? Do not be deceived; neither fornicators, nor idolaters, nor adulterers, nor effeminate, nor homosexuals, nor thieves, nor the covetous, nor drunkards, nor revilers, nor swindlers, will inherit the kingdom of God." (1 Corinthians 6:9-10)

"What we need very badly these days is a company of Christians who are prepared to trust God as completely now as they know they must do at the last day. For each of us the time is surely coming when we shall have nothing but God. Health and wealth and friends and hiding places will all be swept away and we shall have only God. To the man of pseudo faith that is a terrifying thought, but to real faith it is one of the most comforting thoughts the heart can entertain. It would be a tragedy indeed to come to the place where we have no other but God and find that we had not really been trusting God during the days of our earthly sojourn. It would be better to invite God now to remove every false trust, to disengage

*our hearts from all secret hiding places and to bring us out
into the open where we can discover for ourselves whether or
not we actually trust Him. That is a harsh cure for our trou-
bles, but it is a sure one. Gentler cures may be too weak to
do the work. And time is running out on us." —A.W. Tozer*

A T FIRST I thought that maybe there was just something wrong with my television set. Unfortunately,
it didn't take long to realize the problem was much worse
than that.

I had stumbled upon a documentary about a bedridden,
sixteen-year-old boy dying of liver failure. It was obvious
the boy wouldn't be alive much longer. His skin was
bloated and stretched, and the color of his face was such
a sickly yellow that I thought the hues on my television
were out of sync.

The camera soon focused in on the boy's father. It was
all he could do just to hold back the onslaught of endless
tears. The clash of color in their faces was what originally
grabbed my attention. Unlike his father's, the boy's face
was so yellow that it almost looked fake. Like a mask of
some sort.

Something just wasn't right.

The television then began flashing recent photographs
of the boy, taken less than a year before. It looked like
an entirely different person. Those photographs depicted
a young man in the dawn of his life—without a care in
the world—and with little reason to believe that all was

not perfectly well. Unbeknownst to that boy in the photograph, there was a plague on the loose.

Once the telltale symptoms of cancer began to emerge, it wasn't long before the doctors diagnosed his problem. The prognosis was grave. Literally. From that day forward, the boy was no longer concerned about petty things like football, girls, homework, the weekend, or anything else *outside* of him. What wrested his attention from the moment of his diagnosis was the stabbing reality that he had only a year left to live. Maybe only months. Painful months at that.

I felt so sorry for that boy, but I just couldn't get my mind off those recent photographs. I was struck by how his physical appearance so closely resembled the spirituality of many churchgoers today. In reality, his good health was little more than a façade. A false veneer. Fake.

THE PROBLEM WITH SOME CHURCHGOERS

Like many so-called "Christians" in American Christendom today, he looked normal on the outside. Yet somewhere below the surface of the skin, there was a malignant defect eating away at his mortality, and—short of a miracle—it was going to kill him. And soon. There had once been a season when that boy was interested in playing sports, hanging out with friends, and living the good life. But the one thing he was most ignorant of was the one thing that mattered most.

I was reminded about how looks can be so deceiving.

Like the seemingly healthy teenage boy smiling back in those photographs, many churchgoers today are convinced that all is well with their soul. They're so focused on painting the exterior walls of their spiritual façade that they forget about the importance of having a stable foundation. It escapes their notice that "God sees not as man sees, for man looks at the outward appearance, but the LORD looks at the heart."[110] They ignore the telltale symptoms of a heart out of tune with God, convinced they're just as holy as the guy sitting at the other end of the pew.

Like that teenage boy, your days in this world are numbered. Seconds are slipping away fast. Life is little more than a mist in the hands of a sovereign God. The breath you just breathed was borrowed from Him. You inhaled because of His abundant mercy and exhaled because of His grace. And nothing but the sheer pleasure of a relentless God will ever allow you to do so again.

We are not divine. Jesus is. We weren't fashioned by our Maker to obsess over worldly trinkets, but over Christ. We exist in this world for no other reason than to flaunt and parade and proclaim the excellencies of a supreme Lord. It's about time the contemporary Church began to comprehend this simple truth.

Or, as Pastor Rick Warren wrote for the opening sentence of his best-selling book on the Christian life, "It's not about you."[111]

I REALLY HATE THIS CHAPTER

I hate having to write this chapter. I really do. This is far and away my least favorite chapter in the book. Without question. But it's also the most important as well.

It grieves me to know there is even a need for a chapter

110 1 Samuel 16:7
111 Rick Warren, The Purpose Driven Life (Zondervan, 2002), page 17.

like this one. My heart's desire is for believers to worship God with a holy passion and to serve others around them selflessly. But I also know that far too many churches across America look more like a trendy nightclub than anything resembling a New Testament church.

With that said, however, I want to also go on record as saying that I don't believe most of the problems attributed to "Christianity" today are the fault of genuinely saved Christians. Because they're not. The blame for much of the hypocrisy found in contemporary American Christianity lies squarely with the other churchgoers scattered across our pews.

Do you know what I mean?

What I am trying to say is that if we're going to fulfill God's revealed will of discipling His children, then we need to figure out who they are! Frankly, in order for this to occur, we need to determine who are the wheat of God's heavenly harvest and who are the deceived churchgoing tares sown across the landscape of our pews. Unmasking the tares may prove to be both painful and devastating, but doing so is an absolute must if we are going to obey God's command to love our neighbors as ourselves.

A HEARTBREAKING REALITY

I have a friend who attended church faithfully for many years.

She went on short-term mission trips, graduated from a well-known conservative Christian college, and was involved in a young adults' group at her church. If you would have asked me at that time whether she was a true believer or not, I would have answered with a resounding "Yes!"

On the surface, everything about her looked godly. Yet over the next ten years or so, things began to unravel fast. To this day I'm still trying to figure out exactly what happened. She switched churches, moved to a different state, started dating an unbeliever, and today flat-out denies Jesus Christ altogether. She rejects Christ's deity, His atoning work on the cross, and Christianity as a whole.

While exchanging emails some months back, in one of her last replies to me, she stated that she no longer believes in God and doesn't want to talk about any of this ever again.

So I feel compelled to write this chapter.

EVERY CHURCHGOER NEEDS A REGULAR CHECK-UP

Obedient. Ignorant. Disobedient. Complacent.

When it comes to living the Christian life, which of these four best describes the lifestyle of the average person at your church? Yes, it is a loaded question. Not a fair one, you say? Maybe a better way to phrase it would be: Which of these four lifestyles best describes *your own* personal relationship with the Lord?

Well, how about it?

How would you answer that question? Would you say that you've been living a passionate Christian life, the way God intended you to live? Would you describe yourself as being predominantly an obedient, ignorant, disobedient, or a nose-deep-in-the-stinking-pit-of-spiritual-complacency kind of Christian?

I know. Ouch! Too often it's like that for me as well. Yet praise the Lord that He is the God of second chances.

IS OBEDIENCE YOUR PROBLEM?

Are you an *obedient* Christian? Hopefully you are. Being *obedient* to God's Word is the mark of genuine salvation.

Lord willing, you can recall numerous times in your life when you succeeded rather than failed—resisted temptation rather than stumbled—obeyed the Lord rather than rebelled. But if you're anything like the rest of us, there are also more times than you're comfortable admitting to when you didn't obey what you knew was the Lord's will. Nobody's perfect, after all.

But living an *obedient* lifestyle is definitely God's will for you. Obedience is the very emblem of a genuine disciple of Jesus Christ. Faithful obedience to the will and Word of God is precisely what we're to be passionate about here in this world.

But what if your Christian lifestyle couldn't be accurately described as *obedient*? If you're not living a life of God-honoring obedience, could it be that you're deceived by your own *ignorance*?

IS IGNORANCE YOUR PROBLEM?

Most Christians don't like to think of themselves as ignorant when it comes to the things of God, though all of us are to one degree or another.

God is immeasurable, unfathomable, and far beyond all comprehension. We're brutally ignorant when it comes to knowing not only the hidden things of God, but even the revealed jewels found on the pages of Holy Scripture. Yes, we are all biblically ignorant to one degree or another, but this can't be the worst of these four lifestyles when it comes to most churchgoers today, could it?

Undoubtedly, the pursuit of knowing God's Word is critical to growing in our love-relationship with Christ, but the pits of Hell are likely teeming with the souls of men and women who once read, studied, taught, or even memorized what the Bible has to say.

No, ignorance of the Bible is not the biggest problem in most churches today, but it certainly is a formidable one.

That leaves the biggest problem for the average church-goer today as being either *disobedient* or *complacent*.

Is Disobedience Your Problem?

Being disobedient to God is never a good thing. No doubt about it. God hates sin with a holy passion, and, sadly, too often we're disobedient to the commandments of Almighty God. Yet this also cannot be the worst problem in today's American Christianity because most of the churchgoers you know put on a pretty convincing show come Sunday morning.

They guard their tongues from cussing (for the most part) and shout a hearty "Amen!" whenever the preacher calls for abstaining from things like sex, drugs, or drunkenness. They smile and shake your hand ("Good to see you, brother!") when they drop off their kids for Sunday school. Some can even sing the words of "Amazing Grace" from memory.

Thankfully, public disobedience to God is not the main

problem today for most American churchgoers who call themselves *Christian*.

So, if the biggest problem in most American churches today is not ignorance or even disobedience, then that leaves us with plain 'ole *complacency*.

STRIKE THREE—YOU'RE OUT!

It's sad. Really it is. Hundreds of thousands of professing churchgoers today are living joyless lives, drowning in a stagnant pool of spiritual complacency.

Complacency. What does it mean to be spiritually complacent, exactly?

Dictionary.com defines *complacency* as "a feeling of quiet pleasure or security, often while unaware of some potential danger, defect, or the like; self-satisfaction or smug satisfaction with an existing situation."[112] Many of our American churches are packed full of such spiritually complacent, would-be disciples of Jesus Christ.

Oh, not the church you attend—surely—but maybe some of the churches near yours. You know which ones I am talking about. They're the ones you have heard others in your congregation gossiping about. You know the brand of churchgoers I'm describing, don't you? They're the ones generally content with the status quo, apathetic about serving others in the church, and they just can't be bothered with Scripture's command to "test yourselves to see if you are in the faith; examine yourselves!"[113] Never does it cross their unregenerate minds to sit down and count the

---

112 Dictionary.com, http://dictionary.reference.com/browse/complacency (accessed January 4, 2013).
113 2 Corinthians 13:5

cost of whether they are truly in the faith or just another costume-Christian strolling down the broad road of a comfortable religion that leads to spiritual ruin.

I don't suppose you know any churchgoers like that, do you?

PLAYING CATCH WITH GOD

Spiritual complacency is a cruel malady for countless thousands who darken the doors of contemporary Christianity. It isn't all that difficult to pick them out of the crowd, after all.

They're usually the ones who are semi-consistent in attending the main worship service at their church, yet never give a second thought to joining a life group, a Sunday school community group, or even a small-group Bible study during the week. Come Sunday morning they roll out of bed, put on "acceptable" clothes for the occasion, show up to church two minutes before the music starts, sit in the same seat every Lord's Day, and yet couldn't care less about ministering to the needs of those around them. Two seconds after the closing prayer, they're marching toward their cars wondering what's for lunch. They toss God their bone of sacrifice (seventy minutes of church attendance) and assume the Creator of the universe is perfectly satisfied with their offering of sacred crumbs.

"There you go, God. Fetch!"

I don't suppose you know any churchgoers like that, do you?

THE SPIRITUAL NATURES OF TARES AND WHEAT

Tares are not genuine Christians. They think they're saved, but they're really not. Tares are natural-minded, counterfeit churchgoers who lack both biblical repentance and legitimate faith.

They are the ones, for example, who never think twice about purchasing the latest heresy-hardback so they can figure out how to get more and more of their best life now. They're more interested in getting God's stuff than they are in getting more of *God*. Yet that's precisely the problem with tares: they're mainly concerned about what they will be doing over the weekend, not where they'll be two seconds after they're dead.

For the most part, tares are blind to the spiritual darkness of their souls. They are deceived. The thing about tares, however, is that it's sometimes difficult to tell the difference between them and genuine wheat (true Christians). Difficult, that is, until the wheat around them begins to grow, mature, and yield abundant grain. As the wheat begins producing its grain—which is the normal result of worshipping God and serving others—the unfruitful tares inevitably manifest their barren stalks.

WHAT JESUS THINKS ABOUT TARES

In Matthew 13:24-30, Jesus told the following parable about the tares sown among the wheat. He said:

> "The kingdom of heaven may be compared to a man who sowed good seed in his field. But while his men were sleeping, his enemy came and sowed tares among the wheat, and went away. But when the wheat sprouted and bore grain, then the tares became evident also. The slaves of the landowner came and said to him, "Sir, did you not sow good

> seed in your field? How then does it have tares?"
> And he said to them, "An enemy has done this!"
> The slaves said to him, "Do you want us, then, to
> go and gather them up?" But he said, "No; for while
> you are gathering up the tares, you may uproot the
> wheat with them. Allow both to grow together
> until the harvest; and in the time of harvest I will
> say to the reapers, 'First gather up the tares and bind
> them in bundles to burn them up; but gather the
> wheat into my barn.'""

In this parable our Lord explained that there will be
many churchgoing tares scattered both around the world
and throughout the fields of authentic Christianity. In fact,
and lest we miss the point of the lesson, Jesus interpreted
the parable for us a few verses later in Matthew 13:36-43.
He said, "As for the good seed, these are the sons of the
kingdom; and the tares are the sons of the evil one."[114]
In other words, wheat are the children of God (genuine
Christians), and tares are the children of the devil (unbelievers masquerading as professing Christians).

You just cannot get any farther apart on the family tree
than that. Wheat are God's children. Tares call Satan,
"Daddy." Yet both show up for church come Sunday
morning!

CHURCH PEWS AND WEEDY GARDENS

Many churches today have tares sown throughout their
membership.

It's bizarre, really, how the devil's children appear so at

---

114 Matthew 13:38

ease occupying church pews, rubbing shoulders with the worshippers of the God they themselves reject. It can be difficult to distinguish between the genuine and the counterfeit, but not normally. In fact, Jesus said in the parable that the man who owns the field can see (along with his slaves) the difference between the tares and the wheat just fine. Yet notice that the difference in the natures of the plants became apparent at one time in particular: the time when the wheat began to manifest its grain.

My wife and I once had some beautiful Japanese maple trees in our front yard. Every spring, new buds shot forth on their branches. And every autumn, without fail, those blood-red leaves dried out, withered, and fell to the ground.

Over the course of the year, however, some of the branches didn't produce any leaves at all. I never noticed which branches were dead during the cold winter months, because all the leafless branches looked pretty much the same during that time of the year. But as the trees began producing their leaves around the month of March, it became rather easy seeing the difference between the good branches and the bad. So easy, in fact, that I had no problem figuring out which branches should be cut off and which branches were to be left alone.

That is precisely what Jesus is telling us about the wheat (genuine Christians) that will produce its grain, and the tares (unsaved churchgoers) that will remain barren.

Tares are undesirable weeds. Their seeds are actually noxious, "making one feel poisoned with drunkenness, and can cause death."[115] All I'm saying is that you wouldn't want to risk your life by snacking on a bag of roasted tare seeds.

Wheat, on the other hand, produces a grain which nourishes life and is capable of reproducing more wheat and more grain. Spiritually speaking, genuine Christians produce wholesome grain by radically serving God and others, and are capable of reproducing like-minded disciples through the sowing and watering of the Word.

THE FENCE STRADDLERS

Unlike God's children, tares are false converts living a flat-line Christianity.

They are pseudo-Christians who lack a holy pulse. They don't produce any grain because it is not in their unsaved nature to do so. Rather than supporting the wheat, tares steal the soil's nutrients which the wheat needs in order to grow strong and healthy. Sadly, it's like that in hundreds and hundreds of churches across America today. Our churches' limited resources and countless hours of pastoral counseling are wasted on the stony hearts of false converts who feast upon the spiritual manna that was meant for God's children alone.

Such is not always the case, but it occurs more often than God is happy about, I'm sure.

The worst part about all this is that not only should churches not be providing unsaved tares with things like spiritual assurance and pastoral counseling, but we should be warning them to repent and turn to God by faith alone in Jesus. As Christ-loving believers, we shouldn't be

115 Wikipedia.org, www.en.wikipedia.org/wiki/Poison_Darnel (accessed January 4, 2013).

veiling the truth of their depraved condition, but warning them to flee from the wrath to come.

As God's adopted children, we need to reassess our spiritual priorities and inform the tares that they are, indeed, unsaved. That is God's revealed will. It's downright shameful for us to continually ignore their spiritual condition just so we can remain popular, feel more comfortable, or have a *bigger* church. To our own disgrace, many American Christians have made it their personal ministry to do just that.

What do you believe God thinks about all that? Do you think it grieves Him to know that so many of His children are unconcerned about the spiritual welfare of those around them? Do you think it makes God angry? Do you even care all that much if it does?

If you were trapped in a burning building, I bet you'd want someone to tell you about it and do whatever they could to get you out of there. And fast. No doubt the news would initially upset you. But in-your-face truth is not only what you would want to hear, but it's what you'd need to hear. You would be interested in details, not vague generalities. The last thing you would expect your would-be rescuer to do would be to toss you a lukewarm pew so that you're more comfortable when the flames come calling.

Yet that's precisely what much of American Christianity has been doing of late.

THE PROFILE OF A CHURCH-GOING TARE

Simon the Sorcerer is the quintessential example of a New Testament tare. His spiritual hypocrisy is second only to Mr. Iscariot himself.

Immediately after the persecution of the Jerusalem church in Acts chapter eight, Philip the evangelist went down to Samaria and began proclaiming Christ to them. The Samaritans heard the gospel preached, turned from their idolatry and placed their faith in Jesus Christ alone. "Even Simon himself believed; and after being baptized, he continued on with Philip, and as he observed signs and great miracles taking place, he was constantly amazed."[116]

Simon was a man who heard the gospel, believed it intellectually, got baptized, continued along in Philip's ministry, was consistently amazed at all the miracles, and yet was 100% unsaved. Once Simon saw that the Spirit's power came "through the laying on of the apostles' hands, he offered them money, saying, 'Give this authority to me as well, so that everyone on whom I lay my hands may receive the Holy Spirit.'"[117]

Some people want to believe that Simon the Sorcerer was genuinely saved, just immature in his faith. But the apostle Peter didn't believe that at all. In fact, Peter said to him,

> "May your silver perish with you, because you thought you could obtain the gift of God with money! You have no part or portion in this matter, for your heart is not right before God. Therefore repent of this wickedness of yours, and pray the Lord that, if possible, the intention of your heart may be forgiven you. For I see that you are in the gall of bitterness and in the bondage of iniquity."[118]

---

116 Acts 8:13
117 Acts 8:18–19
118 Acts 8:20–23

Notice how Peter described Simon's spiritual condition. He declared Simon's money would "perish" with him, that he had "no part or portion" in the ministry, and that his "heart is not right before God." Peter also told Simon that he believed him to be "in the gall of bitterness and in the bondage of iniquity."

The gall of bitterness?

The bondage of iniquity?

A slave of sin?

In possession of a heart not right before God?

Does that sound like the spiritual status of a genuinely saved Christian to you? No, it most certainly does not. Simon the Sorcerer was a fraud. He was spiritually dead, not biblically immature. He was a believing, baptized, unrepentant, church-attending tare mingling in the fields of early Christianity.

I think it is vitally important for us to understand how Peter ministered to that unsaved, churchgoing tare. His words may seem harsh at first, but they were precisely what Simon needed to hear at the time. In fact, after being radically confronted with the reality of his spiritual bankruptcy, only then did Simon seem more interested in the need for prayer than he was previously about money.

I'm not saying that Simon got saved right then and there, but I am convinced there is a lot to learn from studying how Peter handled that unsaved churchgoer.

HOW DID OUR CHURCHES GET LIKE THIS?

One of the worst tare-sowing campaigns that ever took place was back in the fourth century A.D. It came at the hands of Flavius Theodosius, also known as Theodosius the Great, who was the Roman Emperor from 379 to 395 A.D. While emperor, Theodosius banned all pagan religions and, after issuing a number of decrees, "effectively made Christianity the official state religion of the Roman Empire."[119]

Suddenly, organized Christianity and the Roman Empire were fused together into one gigantic tare factory.

No doubt Theodosius presumed his edict would cause masses of pagans to convert and be saved, but just the opposite occurred. The immediate result was that, on the very next Sunday, thousands of people transitioned into their new Christian religion, dragging their old idolatries, immoralities, and other pagan bents with them. The new churchgoers were unsaved pseudo-converts who were both able and willing to do the devil's bidding whenever he called their number. That's just the plain fact of the matter.

Compulsory Christianity has always proven to be the devil's playground.

Churches all across the world have been dealing with the spawn of those poisonous tare seeds ever since. They go to church and call themselves "Christian," but they're as unregenerate as the devil himself.

Such are the deceived, lukewarm churchgoers about whom Jesus Himself said, "I will spit you out of My mouth."[120] They are the rocky soil in which the seed immediately

---

119 Wikipedia.org, www.en.wikipedia.org/wiki/Theodosius_I (accessed January 4, 2013).
120 Revelation 3:16

"sprang up, because they had no depth of soil."[121] They are the lamp hiding under a basket,[122] the foolish man who built his house on the sand,[123] the ninety-nine sheep that Jesus abandoned in the open country,[124] and the son who said he would go to work in his father's vineyard, "but did not go."[125] They are the foolish virgins who forgot to bring oil for their lamps,[126] and they are the wicked servant who buried his talent in a hole in the ground.[127]

Yes, Jesus taught quite often about the unsaved church-goers who associate themselves with the truth and yet deny its power.

OTHER SIGHTINGS OF TARES IN THE BIBLE

False Christians are the "certain persons" who Jude said "have crept in unnoticed," "have gone the way of Cain," and "are the hidden reefs in your love feasts when they feast with you without fear, caring for themselves."[128] The apostle John said, "They went out from us, but they were not really of us; for if they had been of us, they would have remained with us; but they went out, so that it would be shown that they all are not of us."[129]

The apostle Paul also wrote about these people, saying, "For many walk, of whom I often told you, and now tell you even weeping, that they are enemies of the cross of

---

121 Matthew 13:5
122 See Matthew 5:14-16
123 See Matthew 7:24-47
124 See Luke 15:3-7
125 Matthew 21:30
126 See Matthew 25:1-13
127 See Matthew 25:14-30
128 See Jude 4, 11, and 12
129 1 John 2:19

Christ."[130] Notice Paul used the word "many" and not "some" or "few." Yet the glory will always belong to God. Christ taught this very thing when He concluded the parable about the tares and the wheat, saying,

> "The Son of Man will send forth His angels, and they
> will gather out of His kingdom all stumbling blocks,
> and those who commit lawlessness, and will throw
> them into the furnace of fire; in that place there will
> be weeping and gnashing of teeth. Then the righteous will shine forth as the sun in the kingdom of
> their Father. He who has ears, let him hear."[131]

Question: Do you have spiritual ears to hear?

I Almost Feel Like I Should Apologize

I sure hope I'm not coming across as unloving or overly negative with all this. That is certainly not my intent. I didn't write the Bible; I'm just trying to explain it. I am not trying to be overly controversial, just honest.

It is always painful cleaning a deeply infected wound, but if you don't do it often and thoroughly enough, you may be forced to chop off a leg. Sometimes the truth hurts, and in this politically correct culture of ours, most churchgoers prefer the soft comforts of a lukewarm pew rather than being rescued from the burning building.

I could water down a vial of poisonous cyanide with a glass of the world's cleanest water, but it would still kill you if you drank it.

---

130 Philippians 3:18
131 Matthew 13:41–43

LUKEWARM PEWS

In his book *Crazy Love*, Francis Chan wrote the following about unsaved churchgoers: "Lukewarm people probably drink and swear less than average, but besides that, they really aren't very different from your typical unbeliever. They equate their partially sanitized lives with holiness, but they couldn't be more wrong."[132] He later wrote, "As I see it, a lukewarm Christian is an oxymoron; there's no such thing. To put it plainly, churchgoers who are 'lukewarm' are not Christians. We will not see them in heaven."[133]

Ultimately, wouldn't you rather the churchgoing tares hear it from one of us today, rather than Christ on Judgment Day? Because on that day they will only ever hear, "I never knew you, DEPART FROM ME, YOU WHO PRACTICE LAWLESSNESS." (emphasis mine). [134]

Many Christians assume that it's a wonderful answer to prayer when unbelievers attend their church service on Sunday mornings. And many times it certainly can be. Without question, I am not saying that it's never good to have unsaved seekers attend a church service, because I personally love having unbelievers hear the gospel on a regular and frequent basis. But there's a big difference between repeatedly exposing unsaved people to the gospel and that of welcoming them with open arms into the fellowship.

The point I am trying to make here is that I don't believe the *primary* purpose of our Sunday worship services is about bringing unsaved sinners to church. The apostle Paul put it this way:

132 Francis Chan, <u>Crazy Love</u> (David C. Cook, 2008), page 79.
133 *Ibid,* (David C. Cook, 2008), page 84.
134 Matthew 7:23

"Do not be bound together with unbelievers; for what partnership have righteousness and lawlessness, or what fellowship has light with darkness? Or what harmony has Christ with Belial, or what has a believer in common with an unbeliever...? 'Therefore, come out from their midst and be separate,' says the Lord."[135]

In his first letter to that messed up church in Corinth, Paul wrote, "Do not be deceived: 'Bad company corrupts good morals.'"[136] All I am trying to say is that Great Commission Discipleship starts by having Christians go out into the world to share the gospel with the world, and not necessarily by inviting the world to come to our church services in order to corrupt our good morals.

GREAT COMMISSION DISCIPLESHIP LEADS TO HOLY HATRED

There is perhaps no passage of Scripture that so sufficiently defines what a radical disciple of Jesus Christ looks and acts like as what our Lord taught in Luke 14:26-27. Here is a perfect example of God's revealed will for your life today.

As happened frequently, Jesus was walking from one dusty town to another, and large crowds were trailing in His wake. Some churches today seem overly concerned about filling their pews and stuffing their collection plates, yet have little interest in feeding their lambs Monday through Saturday. Jesus was not such a Shepherd. Rather,

---

135 2 Corinthians 6:14–17
136 1 Corinthians 15:33

He turned around to a particularly large crowd of fickle followers and shouted, "If anyone comes to Me, and does not hate his own father and mother and wife and children and brothers and sisters, yes, and even his own life, *he cannot be My disciple.* Whoever does not carry his own cross and come after Me *cannot be My disciple*" (emphasis mine).[137]

Question: Did you notice that Jesus said "cannot" twice, and that He equated both hatred of other relationships and physical death as the requirement for being a true Christian disciple? I dare you to try that one out at your church's next New Members class and see how it goes.

What Jesus was trying to get His uncommitted followers to understand was that their love for Him needed to be so overwhelmingly compelling that every other human relationship looked almost like hatred when compared to how much they loved Him. If you don't love God's Son that passionately—that radically—Jesus said He would not let you be one of His disciples. He was essentially saying that you're not saved if this isn't true of you.

DOES JESUS WANT BIG CHURCHES?

Many television preachers are becoming multi-millionaires, peddling seed-sowing campaigns that promise health, wealth, and prosperity. But Jesus preached a message requiring hatred and death. Those are two opposing messages, to say the least.

The Son of God wasn't interested in the size of crowds.

---

137 Luke 14:26-27

Popularity was never high on His agenda. He was interested in harvesting wheat, not sowing tares. He was nailed to the cross for the sins of genuine believers, not Christian impersonators. Jesus wanted to make sure that the masses of would-be followers knew exactly who could and who couldn't be one of His disciples. There were no gray areas in the discipleship process as far as the Lord was concerned. The Incarnate God had no taste for lukewarm churchgoers.

It was all or nothing as far as He was concerned.

Hate the world and get crucified for Me—that was Jesus' requirement for being a genuine Christian. My, how far the apple of American Christianity has fallen from the tree of biblical discipleship. In too many churches today, all one has to do to be welcomed into the fellowship is to sign a card, walk an aisle, or pray a prayer—and you're as good as in!

CHECK YOUR PULSE

Have you ever wondered why so many churches today have strayed from Scripture's foundational teachings regarding authentic discipleship? It's baffling to me, really. It is not as though Jesus was vague or unclear about all this.

Please note that Jesus didn't say someone could be His disciple and yet be largely uncommitted or even carnal. No, not at all.

What He said is, you *cannot be My disciple.* You are either a slave of Jesus Christ, or you are not. You're either born again, or you are not. You've either passed from death into life, or you have not. You are either a child of God, or you're the devil's plaything.

It's rather simple and straightforward, after all.

Pastor John MacArthur commented about this highly dangerous trend in contemporary Christianity when he wrote, "Some Christians today seem to take perverse pride in never challenging the lifestyle of anyone who claims to be a believer."[138]

Question: Have you checked your own spiritual pulse lately? Are you passionately in love with Jesus? Do you have a deliberate faith in God? Test yourself.

According to Jesus' statement in that Luke 14:26-27 passage, a true Christian is one who hates and despises everything in this life so far as it hinders them from drawing closer to Him every day.

Does that describe your walk with the Lord? Do you cherish Christ more than anything else this world can offer you? If being a Christian were illegal, would there be enough evidence against you to be found guilty in a court of law? Would there be enough evidence against you even to be charged, let alone tried in court?

JESUS' FAVORITE TOPIC OF CHOICE

Churchgoers around the globe need to understand that this issue of authentic discipleship wasn't some isolated teaching of Jesus. This truly was the common thread to His entire preaching and teaching ministry.

"He was passing through from one city and village to

---

138 John F. MacArthur, Jr., The Gospel According to Jesus (Zondervan, 1994), page 134.

another, teaching, and proceeding on His way to Jerusalem. And someone said to Him, 'Lord, are there just a few who are being saved?' And He said to them, 'Strive to enter through the narrow door; for many, I tell you, will seek to enter and will not be able.'"[139] Contrary to what many church-growth "experts" might have us believe, Jesus said that few churchgoers are entering through the narrow door and are being saved.

What about you? Are you striving to enter through the narrow door of faith in Christ alone? If not, Jesus said that you will seek to enter Heaven and will not be able.

Genuine disciples of Jesus Christ are those who hunger and thirst for righteousness. We experience true satisfaction only when feasting on and obeying God's precious Word. Does that sound like you? Are you hungering and thirsting for the righteousness of God, or is your stomach full from the husks of worldly living?

True servants of Christ don't come to Jesus hoping that God will expand their financial borders or increase their stash of worldly possessions. A true Christian desires to be severed from the bondage of anything which hinders him or her from being molded into the image of God's Son.

Does that sound like you?

A MOMENT OF SELF-EXAMINATION

As I draw this difficult, yet very necessary chapter to a close, allow me to ask you some important questions. Think honestly about how you would answer these. There

---

139 Luke 13:22–24

really is nothing more important in your life than thinking rightly about God and His revealed will for your life.

- Are you more interested in getting God, or in getting what God can give you?

- Do you want Jesus, or just a smiling genie who grants wishes and makes no demands?

- Do you want a holy God, or would a celestial Santa Claus be just as good?

- Would you be perfectly content to inherit a Heaven filled with unimaginable blessings, yet forever empty of God and His glorious presence?

- What exactly is Christianity all about to you? Is it about a right relationship with a holy God, or just about getting a better life in the here and now? (Jesus said, "For what is a man profited if he gains the whole world, and loses or forfeits himself?")[140]

A genuine disciple of Jesus Christ doesn't try to camouflage his faith, but radically alters every human relationship for the glory of God alone. Unlike the tares, genuinely saved disciples of Jesus Christ aren't interested in putting Great Commission Discipleship on cruise control. They willingly embrace death—even by crucifixion—if their Lord so wills it.

Does that describe you? Such radical discipleship is what

---

140 Luke 9:25

Jesus requires of all who claim to be His. There is no room for compromise. He doesn't make exceptions, and He never shows partiality. You're either a *have* or a *have not* when it comes to God's grace. You're either a joyful citizen of Heaven, or you're a mere breath away from Hell's unrelenting embrace.

Which side of Jesus' discipleship-fence are you on right now? In case you are wondering, there are no fence-straddling, almost-Christians in the kingdom of Heaven.

DON'T GET OVER YOUR SALVATION

In his book *The Master Plan of Evangelism*, author Robert E. Coleman wrote about the intense expectations Jesus had for His followers. Coleman wrote, "Jesus expected the men he was with to obey him. They were not required to be smart, but they had to be loyal."[141]

Did Jesus really require obedience and absolute loyalty from those who followed Him? Yes, He did. Here are Jesus' own words concerning loyalty: "He who is not with Me is against Me; and he who does not gather with Me scatters."[142]

Forgive me for being somewhat facetious here, but it sounds like Jesus is saying that if you're not with Him, then you're against Him; if you're not serving Him, then you're fighting against Him. Isn't that what it sounds like to you?

Author and seminary professor Alvin Reid wrote, "The reason many believers today do not attempt to share their

---

141 Robert E. Coleman, The Master Plan of Evangelism (Fleming H. Revell, 2006), page 51.
142 Matthew 12:30

faith is because they have gotten over their salvation."[143] That certainly is a problem for hundreds of thousands in American Christianity today.

Have you gotten over your salvation? Are you on fire with passionate love for Jesus Christ, or is your spiritual gear stuck in neutral? Are you assured of the legitimacy of your salvation, or is it more of a coin-toss at the moment?

The thing about most churches is that they are filled with sinners worshipping a sinless God. Those of us saved by God's amazing grace are radically worshipping the God of our salvation. The rest of the churchgoers—well, they're the ones sitting on lukewarm pews wondering why they haven't been producing any fruit.

Question: Which one are you?

---

143 Alvin Reid, <u>Evangelism Handbook</u> (B&H Publishing Group, 2009), page 24.

CHAPTER EIGHT

THE MESSAGE RARELY SHARED REGARDING GOD'S WILL

". . . teaching them to observe all that I commanded you." (Matthew 28:20)

"And He said to them, 'Go into all the world and preach the gospel to all creation.'" (Mark 16:15)

"Thus it is written, that the Christ would suffer and rise again from the dead the third day, and that repentance for the forgiveness of sins would be proclaimed in His name to all the nations." (Luke 24:46-47)

"Dying to sin is the life of repentance. The very day a Christian turns from sin he must enjoin himself a perpetual fast. The eye must fast from impure glances. The ear must fast from hearing slanders. The tongue must fast from oaths. The hands must fast from bribes. The feet must fast from the paths of a harlot. And the soul must fast from the love of wickedness. This turning from sin implies a notable change. There is a change wrought in the heart. The flinty

heart has become fleshly. Satan would have Christ prove his deity by turning stones into bread. Christ has wrought a far greater miracle in making stones become flesh. In repentance Christ turns a heart of stone into flesh." —Thomas Watson

WHILE I WAS preaching at a local jail, one Hispanic man in particular had been attending the chapel services regularly and for many consecutive weeks. I had high hopes that God would remove the veil of unbelief, open his heart, and save his soul. I have that hope still today.

I never learned his name, but he was an active gang member with multiple tattoos all over his arms, neck, and face. Not exactly the kind of guy you hope your daughter brings home to meet the parents, if you know what I mean.

For weeks he had been coming to my chapel services and seemed to be responding positively to what I had been teaching from the Scriptures, though he'd certainly shown no desire to surrender to the lordship of Christ.

During one particular chapel service, I was preaching from John 14:6 where Jesus declared, "I am the way, and the truth, and the life; no one comes to the Father but through Me." I was wrapping up my message, pleading with the men to be reconciled to God. I was also trying to make it quite clear, however, that they cannot merely add Jesus to their own collection of filthy, self-righteous rags, for the Savior is not on add-on, charm, or lucky rabbit's foot. They needed to come with empty hands, begging God to do it all for them.

I explained how this statement from Jesus was

exceptionally exclusive, prohibiting all other religions from reaching the one true God.

"You can't get to God through Buddha, Muhammad, or your own self-righteousness," I was telling them. It was at that precise moment that this guy jumped out of his chair, crumpled the Scripture, threw it on the ground, and yelled, "I'm outta here! He said I can't come through Muhammad!" He then marched past me with such a wicked scowl that I still get goose bumps just thinking about it. Pounding on the barred door so that the guards would let him out, he yelled through the reinforced glass, "Get me outta here! He said I can't get to Heaven through Muhammad!"

No matter how often something like that happens while I am preaching, it never fails to freak me out.

I grieved (after first breathing a sigh of relief) over his soul as he walked out that door. But I was at least content with the fact that he had grasped the exclusive claims of Jesus Christ when it comes to salvation. I then used that man's abrupt exit as one final illustration to the men about coming to God on His terms alone. I warned those men about their desperate need to repent of their sin and turn to God by faith alone in Jesus Christ.

THE GOSPEL, THE WHOLE GOSPEL, AND NOTHING BUT THE GOSPEL

When considering the many facets of Jesus Christ's Great Commission mandate, every one of them is necessary and important. None are more critical, however, than making quite certain we get the content of the gospel message right.

Teaching and believing the unaltered gospel message is

essential for rightly determining God's will for your life today.

There are a few cults exceptionally active at going door-to-door, peddling their theology, but few rise above the tide called "heresy."

Dozens of aid organizations spend untold millions of dollars in overseas humanitarian work—waving the banner of Christianity—yet you'd be hard pressed to locate one native converted according to the biblical definition of the Way.

Sadly, hundreds of American preachers stand behind their pulpits each Sunday trying to meet sinners' *felt needs* rather than proclaiming the one message that would cure their greatest need of all. Such pastors are band-aid preachers, offering sinners gauze for their splinters when the real problem is a rebellious heart bent toward the love of sin. Worse yet, it appears that almost anyone can get a job as a television evangelist, so long as they write a bestselling novel catering to the fantasies of an undiscerning audience with their credit cards handy.

No, it's not more programs or activities or gimmicks that are needed in the church today. What is needed, however, is the biblical gospel of grace alone through repentant faith alone.

So that begs an important question: According to the Great Commission passages themselves, what exactly is the message Jesus said we should proclaim to all the nations?

A TIMELESS MESSAGE

At the time Christ ascended through the clouds, there were as yet no New Testament books written. In fact, the first New Testament book was not penned until some fifteen years after Jesus ascended into Heaven. (The book of Revelation, which was the final book of the Bible written, wasn't penned until roughly five decades later). The revealed gospel message was, at that time, contained in what is commonly called the Old Testament, and the words of Jesus Christ Himself, which truly are one and the same.

Gospel truth is the same yesterday, today, and forever, whether it is found in the older or newer testaments.

When we examine the actual Great Commission texts, there are relatively few parts that provide details about the specific content of the gospel message itself. There are portions which explain what to do with the disciples in general (baptize and teach), where we are to preach the gospel geographically, how Christians receive power to share that message, and even that Christ will be with us as we go. Yet there are precious few statements from the Lord that specifically describe the content of the gospel message itself.

So what exactly were the disciples supposed to tell people?

CONTENT IS KING

Take a fresh look at these Great Commission passages and reintroduce yourself to the content of this simple—yet profound—gospel message.

- "...teaching them to observe all that I commanded you." (Matthew 28:20)

- "And He said to them, 'Go into all the world and preach the gospel to all creation.'" (Mark 16:15)

- "Thus it is written, that the Christ would suffer and rise again from the dead the third day, and that repentance for the forgiveness of sins would be proclaimed in His name to all the nations." (Luke 24:46-47)

From these passages, we see that Matthew tells us we are to be "teaching" the disciples "all that I commanded you." Mark says we are to "preach the gospel," and Luke informs us that what is to be "proclaimed" is "repentance for the forgiveness of sins." In other words, Jesus commands us to preach and teach the gospel, which is a message requiring repentance for the forgiveness of sins.

On the surface, it may not seem like a lot of substance overall. Yet as we dig a bit deeper, we strike gospel oil.

According to the Lord's revealed will for the local church, the gospel we are to proclaim is everything that Christ taught, which is further summarized as "repentance for the forgiveness of sins." In fact, repentance is the very first subject Jesus preached about when He began His public ministry.

He said, "The time is fulfilled, and the kingdom of God is at hand; repent and believe in the gospel."[144] This is particularly significant when compared to most gospel presentations delivered in contemporary Christianity today. A disturbing trend reveals that, generally speaking, the message

---

144 Mark 1:15

peddled across our nation is so watered-down that not only is repentance glossed over with little more than a bashful apology, but in many cases it is absent altogether.

Author Randy Newman wrote, "If we think that the gospel is simply a good deal that any reasonable person would accept, we'll not only be amazed at how many people turn it down, but we may actually distort the message in the process of proclaiming it."[145]

This is regrettably the case in many Christian circles today.

THE DEVIL'S ERASURE

I recently collected a substantial number of doctrinal statements of faith from conservative, reformed, and evangelical seminaries, churches, and para-church ministries. I wanted to see where they each stood theologically on this critical issue of repentance. I must confess that by the time I finished reading them, I was rather discouraged.

The apple of biblical repentance has fallen far from the tree of grace. This is certainly not God's will for our churches today.

Practically all of the doctrinal statements were healthy as far as their definitions of the Godhead, the inerrancy of Scripture, the sufficient work of Christ on the cross, eschatology, and the necessity of faith are all concerned. However, in the vast majority of them (yes, the vast majority!), key words like *repent* or *turn* or *repentance* were missing altogether.

Why does this occur when the teachings of the Old Testament, of Jesus Christ, and even the New Testament

---

145 Randy Newman, <u>Questioning Evangelism</u> (Kregel Publications, 2004), page 35.

writers speak about the necessity of repentance so very often?

It appears that Satan has taken an eraser to many of our statements of faith. We have once again become ignorant of his schemes. As a result, we can't do what the writer of Hebrews suggested:

> "Therefore leaving the elementary teachings about Christ, let us press on to maturity, *not laying again a foundation of repentance from dead works* and of faith toward God, of instructions about washings and laying on of hands, and the resurrection of the dead and eternal judgment. And this we will do if God permits" (emphasis mine).[146]

REPENTANCE IS GOOD NEWS, NOT BAD NEWS

The word "gospel" means good news. Jesus told us to teach and preach the gospel to all creation. Our Christian message to the world is ultimately one of good news. An imperative aspect of the gospel message—according to Jesus Himself—is that forgiveness of sins is directly tied to biblical repentance. Therefore, the Great Commission gospel seed that we are to sow among the soils of the nations, in order to make genuine disciples of Jesus Christ, is the spectacular news of biblical repentance.

As Christians, we're to be about the business of preaching and teaching the gospel, the whole gospel, and nothing but the gospel. We're not given the liberty of adding anything to the gospel, and we are certainly not

---

146 Hebrews 6:1–3

permitted to leave *undesirable* bits and pieces out of it. The gospel is what it is. Period.

Jesus was not crucified on a watered-down cross, and the cup He drank on our behalf was not brimmed with watered-down wrath, either.

The gospel message is simple and straightforward. It's not blurry, fuzzy, or open for debate as to its cultural relevance. The gospel of Jesus Christ contains the imperishable truth that if a person does not repent of their sin, then they don't have forgiveness of sin.

Repentance is not a difficult doctrine to comprehend (even for young children), and Jesus was not speaking in parables when He insisted on it. Repentance is not an appalling topic for sinners to hear, but it is certainly disgraceful for Christians to water it down or—worse yet—ignore it altogether!

DRINKING WATERED-DOWN CHRISTIANITY

Essentially, what many in contemporary Christianity have done is attempt to extract the medicinal qualities from the bottle of salvation and still label it the cure for sin. Churchgoers have been force-fed a steady diet of spiritual placebos packaged with *Just believe!* In doing so, they've been forsaken and forced to drink the same bitter dregs as before. Hearers who haven't become doers of the Word have been tricked into thinking that they're saved merely because they believe a few facts about Jesus, the Bible, or Christianity in general.

Scripture provides many warnings for all those who do not repent of their sin. For instance, the apostle Paul wrote, "Because of your stubbornness and unrepentant heart, you are storing up wrath for yourself in the day of wrath and revelation of the righteous judgment of God."[147] Unrepentant hearers not only don't have forgiveness of their sins, but they are actually storing up for themselves God's wrath in the day of their final judgment.

Since the obligation of repentance is the plain gospel truth, why do so many Christians insist on leaving it out of their gospel presentations and doctrinal statements of faith? Apparently, they don't believe repentance is altogether necessary for the forgiveness of sins. But if that's true, then Jesus was either Scripturally ignorant or He was a devious liar in cahoots with the devil, because He commanded that "repentance for the forgiveness of sins would be proclaimed in His name to all the nations."[148]

Since the gospel of repentance is good news, deleting it from our evangelistic message is to withhold that which is good, profitable, and necessary for salvation. To assure people of salvation while at the same time not commanding them to repent of their sin isn't being kind—it's heresy!

In reality, it is preaching a different gospel altogether. The apostle Paul wrote to the Galatians, saying, "As we have said before, so I say again now, if any man is preaching to you a gospel contrary to what you received, he is to be accursed!"[149]

Accursed heretics, in case you didn't already know, will not inherit the kingdom of Heaven. To believe or

---

147 Romans 2:5
148 Luke 24:47
149 Galatians 1:9

proclaim an unbiblical gospel is definitely not God's will for your life.

THE MESSAGE IS REPENTANCE— NOT RUDENESS

I was visiting my in-laws one afternoon when their next-door neighbor came over for coffee while his children played with mine in the backyard. After lunch we chatted around the table about this, that, and the other thing. After an hour or so, I decided to transition the conversation into the spiritual realm once the present topic of discussion had ended.

During lunch, I learned that the man was in the medical profession and that he was once offered a job as a medical nurse at a local prison. I told him about my being a religious volunteer at a local jail and how I simply love asking the prisoners a particular question about religion. Everyone has an opinion on the subject of this question, and the answers I receive are always—without exception—downright fascinating.

I asked him, "What do you think happens to a person's soul immediately after they die?"

He wasn't offended by my question in the least bit, confessing he'd considered the issue many times before, seeing as he is in the medical field. He said that he believed in a real Heaven and Hell and that he was raised in a church-attending home, but he hadn't been to church in years. He then added that he hoped he was going "north," not "south."

I asked what he thought the requirement was for entrance

into Heaven. After some silent consideration, he said it had to have something to do with the Ten Commandments. I agreed, in that it had *something* to do with God's holy Law. That is, something with regards to turning away from self-righteousness and surrendering to God through faith in Jesus Christ alone.

We had a blessed conversation thereafter. My father-in-law and I were then able to explain to him the biblical gospel of God's grace through repentant faith alone. When the conversation was finally over, we were all still friends. Yet from that moment forward, he now knew what the Bible truly teaches about what happens immediately after someone dies.

YOU CAN NOT REPENT
WITHOUT GENUINE FAITH

There is a kind of faith that genuinely leads to salvation, but there's also counterfeit faith that is truly dead by itself. "Even so faith, if it has no works, *is dead*, being by itself" (emphasis mine).[150]

In the Great Commission passage of Luke 24:47, the Greek word translated "repentance" is "metanoian." *Metanoian* comes from two separate words. The prefix *meta* means *after*, and implies change. The second Greek word, *noeo* means *to perceive with the mind*. *Metanoian*, then, literally means "to perceive afterwards...hence signifies to change one's mind or purpose, always, in the N.T., involving a change for the better."[151]

Repentance, then, means doing a 180-degree turn-around

---

150 James 2:17
151 W.E. Vine, <u>Expository Dictionary of New Testament Words</u> (Fleming H. Revell Company, 1966), page 279-280.

in your *thinking*, which inevitably results in a 180-degree transformation in the *externals* of your lifestyle. It is the absolute opposite of what a person used to think, believe, and do about practically all things moral and spiritual, concerning both themselves and the God of the Bible.

A Beautiful Ten-Letter Word

Repentance is a rich and beautifully significant word. It's so intertwined with the substance of saving faith that if you were to try and separate the two, you'd be left with unrecognizable rags of a rancid religion. A person cannot truly repent without possessing true faith. Moreover, a person cannot have true saving faith without experiencing biblical repentance.

For example:

- Would a person ever suddenly reject, forsake, and abandon everything they always assumed to be true, unless they had a catastrophic, 180-degree change in their thinking?

- Would a person forsake and turn away from sin, lust, self-righteousness, and everything else contrary to the will of God unless they truly believed that what they had done was thoroughly wrong and now they wanted only what is entirely right?

- Would a person ever turn away from their love of sin unless they were first totally convinced that their old ways were wicked and they now desired only the things of God?

Of course not. That drastic of a change in lifestyle would first require an equally drastic change in thinking.

It is for this reason that repentance and faith go hand-in-hand. Or as James, our Lord's half-brother, wrote, "Even so faith, if it has no works, is dead, being by itself."[152]

Pastor Mark Dever wrote:

> "Repentance and this kind of belief, or faith, or reliance, are really two sides of the same coin. It's not like you can go for the basic model (belief) and add repentance at a later point when you want to get really holy. No! Repent is what you do if you really start thinking this way and believing Jesus with your life. Any purported belief without change is nothing but a base counterfeit."[153]

J.I. Packer went so far as to say,

> "Evangelism is the issuing of a call to turn, as well as to trust; it is the delivering, not merely of a divine invitation to receive a Saviour, but of a divine command to repent of sin. And there is no evangelism where this specific application is not made."[154]

ARE YOU A RELIGIOUS SCHIZO?

Many churchgoers in American Christianity today are religious schizophrenics. They're suffering from a sin disorder characterized by a disintegration of thought processes and

---

152 James 2:17
153 Mark Dever, The Gospel & Personal Evangelism (Crossway Books, 2007), page 42.
154 J.I. Packer, Evangelism & the Sovereignty of God (InterVarsity Press, 1961), page 40.

bizarre delusions. They are walking around thinking they're Christian, but—in reality—they are deceived. Religiously delusional, if you will.

Blinded by the corruption of their own hearts and minds, they have eyes to see, but they do not see. They have ears to hear, but they cannot hear the plain truth of the gospel. They claim to have saving faith, but they lack biblical repentance. "They profess to know God, *but by their deeds they deny Him*, being detestable and disobedient and worthless for any good deed" (emphasis mine).[155]

Unless God grants them repentance for the forgiveness of sins, they'll be swept away by the tide of wrath they have been storing up for themselves in the coming day of wrath. And there will be no one to blame but themselves.

GOD'S WILL IS REPENTANT FAITH

Repentance is the marriage partner of faith. (They both say, "I do.")

Repentance and faith walk the same line, lead to the same destination, and will never be separated. In fact, except for those either too young or of a mental condition making them incapable of understanding sin and their need of the gospel, there will not be a single person in Heaven who had not repented of his or her sin and turned to Christ while in this life.

Repentance means that you're turning away from the yoke of idolatrous sin and rebellion and are turning to God by faith in His Son Jesus Christ for the forgiveness of your sins. It is the sovereign and free gift of a changed

---

155 Titus 1:16

mind resulting in a changed lifestyle. God saves sinners according to His matchless grace, and He does this through the means of repentant faith.

Repentance is not a works-based righteousness any more than mere faith is.

REPENTANCE AND FAITH

One of the greatest passages in Scripture teaching this fundamental doctrine is found in Mark 1:14-15. It says, "Now after John had been taken into custody, Jesus came into Galilee, preaching the gospel of God, and saying, 'The time is fulfilled, and the kingdom of God is at hand; *repent and believe in the gospel*'" (emphasis mine). Notice that the text says Jesus was preaching the gospel of God, and what Jesus declared needs to be done is for hearers to repent and believe.

Jesus was not teaching a works-based pathway to salvation. He was simply exhorting people to submit themselves to a new Lord by turning away from sin and believing in God. This miraculous recipe for salvation is found throughout the pages of New Testament Scripture.

HEAVEN IS AT HAND

For example, in Matthew 3:2, John the Baptist cried out in the wilderness, "Repent, for the kingdom of heaven is at hand."

When Jesus began His public ministry only days thereafter, the first words He expressed were no different in either substance or brevity, for our Lord pronounced, "Repent, for the kingdom of heaven is at hand."[156]

WHAT IS WRONG WITH THAT CITY?

As Jesus traveled from city to city, He was constantly running into people who enjoyed the fringe benefits of His ministry, yet were unwilling to surrender to Him as Lord of their life. "Then He began to denounce the cities in which most of His miracles were done, because they did not repent. 'Woe to you, Chorazin! Woe to you, Bethsaida! For if the miracles had occurred in Tyre and Sidon which occurred in you, they would have repented long ago in sackcloth and ashes.'"[157]

In Matthew 12:41, Jesus confessed that, during the final judgment, the people in Heaven who repented will point the finger and condemn those who didn't repent. "The men of Ninevah will stand up with this generation at the judgment," He said, "and will condemn it because they repented at the preaching of Jonah; and behold, something greater than Jonah is here."

When Jesus sent out His disciples in pairs, He gave them a particular message to preach, and it had nothing to do with *Just believe!* Mark 6:12 tell us that "They went out and preached that men should repent."

RANDOM ACTS OF NATURE?

There was a time when people approached Jesus and told Him about some Jews who'd been murdered while in the

---

156 Matthew 4:17
157 Matthew 11:20–21

very act of offering their animal sacrifices. Rather than condemning the incident altogether, Jesus used it as a picture for what needed to be done by all people. He said, "I tell you no, but that unless you repent, you will all likewise perish."[158]

Immediately after that statement, Jesus then asked those same people what they thought about a certain tower that came crashing down, killing eighteen people. He asked them whether or not they thought those people were worse sinners than all the rest. Rather than waiting for a reply, He emphatically announced, "I tell you no, but that unless you repent, you will all likewise perish."[159]

Notice, Jesus issued an identical statement regarding people who were murdered during religious worship and those who were killed during seemingly random mishaps of nature. But what is interesting is that although Jesus used the same Greek word for "repent" in both cases, He altered the tense of the verb.

In Luke 13:3, Jesus used "repent" in the present imperative mood, which means to repent with ongoing, continuous force. Yet in verse five He used an aorist, which means that "repent" is a one-time, single, and decisive action.

In other words, in verse three Jesus was telling the people that they needed to keep on repenting, over and over again. In verse five He said that there needed to be a one-time, decisive act of repentance. We see, then, that Jesus was teaching about the need for the critical act of repenting for salvation once and for all, as well as the daily, ongoing repenting of sin throughout one's lifetime.

158 Luke 13:3
159 Luke 13:5

WHEN GOD REJOICES

Jesus also taught that God Himself experiences great joy when people repent of their sin.

He said, "There is joy in the presence of the angels of God over one sinner who repents."[160] God is the only one in the presence of the angels, so it is the Father's joy which Jesus spoke of.

IF IT AIN'T BROKE, DON'T TRY TO FIX IT

When the Church was born on the Day of Pentecost in the second chapter of Acts, Peter preached a sermon in which his listeners were pierced in their hearts, crying out and asking what they should do. Rather than respond with *Just believe*, Peter immediately told them, "Repent, and each of you be baptized in the name of Jesus Christ for the forgiveness of your sins."[161] Here Peter was essentially saying the very same thing that Jesus commanded in the Great Commission passage: that repentance is necessary for the forgiveness of sins.

If there is no repentance, then there has been no forgiveness of sin.

Contemporary proponents of a watered-down gospel probably have a major problem with the content of Peter's sermon. After all, never once does he even mention the word *faith*. The reason he didn't feel the need to separate faith from repentance is because they are really opposite sides of the same coin. There is no repenting without also having true faith. The two go together.

---

160 Luke 15:10
161 Acts 2:38

Peter didn't revise the content of his gospel presentation at his very next public preaching opportunity, either. While speaking to a large group of people in Solomon's Portico, Peter exhorted his listeners with, "Therefore, repent and return, so that your sins may be wiped away."[162] Peter was saying that if a person does not repent of their sin, then their sin wouldn't be wiped away. In other words, they're still dead in their trespasses and sin.

Repentance is absolutely necessary for salvation, and the Bible repeats this holy theme time and time again.

It Isn't Magic

While rebuking Simon the Sorcerer in Acts 8:21-23, Peter told him, "You have no part or portion in this matter, for your heart is not right before God. Therefore repent of this wickedness of yours, and pray the Lord that, if possible, the intention of your heart may be forgiven you." Peter said that a heart not right before God is a heart that has never repented of its sin.

Once again, Peter correlated the necessity of repentance in order to receive forgiveness.

But please don't assume for a moment that repentance is a *work* or an *effort* or an *achievement* that we must accomplish in order to right ourselves with God. On the contrary, repentance is an unmerited gift from God in the same way that faith is.

It is God's grace that saves people, not human effort.

---

162 Acts 3:19

REPENTANCE IS A GIFT FROM GOD

For example, after Peter explained to the Jewish Christians back in Jerusalem about what God did for Cornelius and his entire Gentile household, the apostles and other circumcised believers then confessed, "Well then, *God has granted to the Gentiles* also the repentance that leads to life" (emphasis mine).[163]

God showers people with His amazing grace by granting them repentant faith to believe, leading to eternal life.

Moreover, while instructing Timothy about the necessary qualifications for church leadership, the apostle Paul wrote:

> "The Lord's bondservant must not be quarrelsome, but be kind to all, able to teach, patient when wronged, with gentleness correcting those who are in opposition, if perhaps *God may grant them repentance* leading to the knowledge of the truth, and they may come to their senses and escape from the snare of the devil, having been held captive by him to do his will" (emphasis mine).[164]

Repentance, Paul says, is granted by God. It is not exercised through the efforts of ensnared and enslaved humanity.

EVEN INTELLECTUALS MUST THINK AGAIN

While preaching to the philosophers and other intellectuals on Mars Hill in Athens, the apostle Paul declared, "Therefore having overlooked the times of ignorance, God

---

163 Acts 11:18
164 2 Timothy 2:24-25

is now declaring to men that all people everywhere should repent."[165]

Repentance is a requirement that God demands of all people everywhere, whether they are Jew or Gentile.

THE MAIN THEME AT CHURCH SERVICES

After assembling the Ephesian elders in order to express his final farewell, the apostle Paul urged the other pastors (elders) to consider the ministry he had with them for a period of three years as their pastor. What did Paul preach and teach about over the course of those three years? "I did not shrink from declaring to you anything that was profitable, and teaching you publicly and from house to house, solemnly testifying to both Jews and Greeks of repentance toward God and faith in our Lord Jesus Christ."[166]

Paul said that it didn't matter what the venue was or what environment he found himself teaching in. He was determined only to relay anything that was profitable, which to him meant repentance and faith.

IT IS GOOD ENOUGH FOR KINGS

While being handcuffed and summoned to appear before King Agrippa, the apostle Paul was granted the opportunity to share his personal testimony in Acts 26:19-20. He confessed,

> "So, King Agrippa, I did not prove disobedient
> to the heavenly vision, but kept declaring both to
> those of Damascus first, and also at Jerusalem and

---

165 Acts 17:30
166 Acts 20:20-21

then throughout all the region of Judea, and even to the Gentiles, that they should repent and turn to God, performing deeds appropriate to repentance."

HOW THE ELECT GET SAVED

Writing in his first epistle about the patience of our heavenly Father and His desire for the elect to be saved, Peter wrote, "The Lord is not slow about His promise, as some count slowness, but is patient toward you, not wishing for any to perish but for all to come to repentance."[167]

THERE MUST BE SOMETHING WRONG WITH US

Ultimately, although repentance may be an unpopular topic in many contemporary American churches, it remains a biblical one. Repentance is required for the forgiveness of sin. A person is never saved by God and then allowed to repent at a later date when they feel a subjective need to rededicate their faith, or never at all.

Repentance assumes the fact that something is terribly wrong, requiring immediate correction. In truth, sin is separating us from our God. Without the turning from sin to God, there is no hope of ever receiving forgiveness of sins and escaping the wrath that is to come.

To know the revealed will of God is to understand our need to repent of sin. God's revealed will for all people everywhere is that we repent of our sin and turn to God by faith alone in Jesus Christ for the forgiveness of our sins.

---

167 1 Peter 3:9

The gospel of Jesus Christ really is that simple.

Question: Have you ever repented of your sin?

THE FACE OF UNREPENTANT CHRISTIANITY

Bus stops are great places for sharing the gospel, because sinners keep coming and going all day long. Most of them are usually sitting down and won't walk away—even if they don't like what you have to say—because they don't want to miss their bus. Sometimes I think God created public transportation just so believers would have a great place to share the gospel.

A while back, I went out witnessing at one of the local bus stops in my hometown. I walked up to a woman who was sitting on a bench, handed her a *Ticket To Heaven* gospel tract, and asked her which ticket she thought she'd be holding if she died that very night.

One side of this particular tract says "Ticket to Heaven," and the other side says "Ticket to Hell." She looked at the Heaven side first and quickly smiled at the genius of it. That side appealed to her quite nicely indeed. "Oh, I'm a Christian," she added. "I go to such-and-such church just around the corner. Heaven is where I'll end up for sure!"

She then turned the tract over, saw the fiery red flames and the word "HELL" in bold letters, and got all bent out of shape. She proceeded to then give me an earful about why people like me shouldn't go around cramming their religion down other people's throats.

I tried my best to calm her down, but she must have been having a really bad day. Smiling, I let her vent a few more minutes. Once she calmed down, I informed her that God commands His children to talk to all kinds of people—including religious churchgoers like her—about things like sin and judgment, so that if they refuse to repent of their sin and embrace Christ, they'll have no excuse on Judgment Day when they're cast into the lake of fire.

Suffice it to say my comments did not cheer her up. Not in the slightest.

Question: What was wrong with that woman's religion?

Answer: She was a disillusioned churchgoing tare sown among God's wheat. A false convert living the lifestyle of a pseudo-Christian. She liked the idea of going to Heaven (doesn't everyone?), but the thought of turning from her cherished sin was a repulsive suggestion. She enjoyed Christianity; she just preferred a fairy-tale form of it that didn't include a real place called Hell. So dear was sin to her heart that she would have rather parted with her tongue than say goodbye to pride.

WHY WOULD ANYONE LEAVE REPENTANCE OUT OF THE GOSPEL?

If you are anything like me, you've often wondered what could be so intimidating that it would hinder a genuine Christian from being passionately obedient to the revealed will of God when it comes to sharing the gospel.

Occasionally, the scarcity of evangelism has to do with a lack of Bible knowledge, or maybe just plain ignorance. But if we were honest with ourselves we'd probably all agree that it usually boils down to *irrational fear*. We have a practical fear of man and not a high enough view of God. When it comes to fulfilling God's revealed will of Great Commission Discipleship, too often we cower before depraved men rather than tremble before a holy God.

Instead of passionately worshipping God and viewing the world as a fertile mission field, we regularly exchange the divine nudging of evangelism for other spiritual acts of worship (like studying the Bible or praying more about sharing our faith), and we hope that God won't mind too much if we exchange the two. But I'm pretty sure He knows what we're doing.

It is a whole lot easier, after all, to pray to God about our loved ones then it is to actually speak to those loved ones about the God who made them.

Evangelism Is Like a Vapor

Although acts of religious worship such as singing songs of praise and fellowshipping with likeminded believers are quite necessary and carry tremendous spiritual blessings, Jesus also commanded us to preach the gospel to all creation. Making disciples involves the necessity of exhorting sinners to repent for the forgiveness of their sins. You'll have all of eternity to fellowship with other believers in sinless glory, but you have precious few moments on Earth to witness to the lost.

Use your minutes wisely.

In fact, once you die and pass through Heaven's gates, the one thing you will never again do in eternity future is meet someone who doesn't know Jesus Christ as their personal Lord and Savior. Never again will you have the privilege of telling a sinner the good news of the gospel, pleading with them to turn from sin and embrace Christ as Lord of their life.

The ministries of local evangelism and foreign missions will last only as long as the vapor of your life.

There is no greater message than that people may be immediately and forever liberated from the slavery of sin by the free gift of a compassionate God. Let us be sure to obey our Lord's command to preach and teach the gospel of repentance for the forgiveness of sin to all the nations of this world.

Beloved, this is most certainly God's will for your life, both today and tomorrow.

CHAPTER NINE

THE PROBLEM WITH BEING 99% OBEDIENT TO GOD'S REVEALED WILL

"Let your heart therefore be wholly devoted to the LORD our God, to walk in His statutes and to keep His commandments, as at this day." (1 Kings 8:61)

"The notion that faith is nothing more than believing a few biblical facts caters to human depravity." —John MacArthur

THIS IS BY no means the chapter I was planning to write at this point in the book. I would much prefer to dive right into the next one. I'm excited about the upcoming, highly controversial topic found there. But I also know that the very thought of "divine persecution" causes many Christians to fidget and squirm in their theological seats. And since that is the case, it deserves a thorough introduction.

So buckle up and hold on tight.

An Event That Set the World on Fire

Once Stephen was murdered for his Christian faith in Acts chapter seven, life in the city of Jerusalem exploded into unbridled chaos.

For the most part, the early church had been experiencing heavenly bliss up to that day. Miraculous signs and wonders were being performed at the hands of the apostles, the fellowship among like-minded believers was sweet, the church was devoting itself to the apostles' teaching, and the redeemed were experiencing favor among all the people. Aside from sitting under the earthly ministry of Christ Himself, living in Jerusalem at that time must have been the closest thing to Heaven on Earth. More eternally significant than anything else was the fact that the "Lord was adding to their number day by day those who were being saved."[168]

What a fantastic time in redemptive history it must have been!

No doubt the prolific and gruesome persecution the church in Jerusalem experienced right after Stephen's murder was a bit of a shocker. The disciples must have assumed the Lord would just continue to bless them with love, joy, peace, and the salvation of many souls. Apparently the Lord had other plans.

But why?

Why would God do that? Why did God allow His children to be brutally persecuted like they were, especially since He'd been blessing their evangelistic zeal for nearly two years up to that point? The answer to such questions

168 Acts 2:47

regarding the harsh persecution of Christians, frankly, may not be something you've ever considered.

The answer, I believe, all boils down to God's sovereign reaction to the early church's spiritual complacency, ignorance, and lack of radical obedience to the clear commandments of His Son.

THE DEVIL'S BEAST OR THE LORD'S PRODDING STICK?

The devil can't even sneeze without first obtaining God's permission to do so.

Have you ever thought about that? God is in absolute sovereign control over every detail in this universe, especially the safety, wellbeing, and prosperity of His redeemed people. God does not tempt anyone to sin, but there are occasions in life when He allows us to be tested in order to reveal the substance of our faith.

Just ask Job.

Personally, I'll never forget how God described Job because I always recall the acronym, BUFT. We read in Job 1:8, "The LORD said to Satan, 'Have you considered My servant Job? For there is no one like him on earth, a blameless and upright man, fearing God and turning away from evil.'" Job was a BUFT man (Blameless, Upright, Fearing God, Turning away from evil). Why God ever allowed the devil to harm a BUFT guy like Job, I suppose we'll have to wait until we get to glory to find out.

Have you ever found yourself in a place where God allowed you to be thoroughly tested and, from your vantage point, almost cruelly so? Rarely are we ever grateful during (or after) times like that. I don't know about you, but too often I'm more prone to accuse others and shake my fist toward the heavens before ever looking to my own sin as the reason for my suffering.

Have you ever experienced anything like that? I'm sure you probably have.

Ever wondered why God didn't incarcerate the devil (and all the other demons, for that matter) in chains like He did with the "angels who did not keep their own domain, but abandoned their proper abode, He has kept in eternal bonds under darkness for the judgment of the great day"?[169] No doubt it would have made our lives a lot easier if He had. But God had His reason for not doing so.

Remember when Jesus warned Peter, saying, "Simon, Simon, behold, Satan has demanded permission to sift you like wheat"?[170] Scripture doesn't tell us much about Peter's reaction at that point, but I assume he probably responded with something like, "And you told him to take a hike, right, Lord?"

You see, everything is off limits to that sinful slanderer unless God allows it to be otherwise. Satan needs divine permission. Satan needs God's permission. The devil is God's devil. The devil and his demonic army are formidable enemies of humanity—to be sure—but too often we ascribe more power to the devil than he actually has.

Have you ever been guilty of doing that? I know I have.

---

169 Jude 1:6
170 Luke 22:31

DON'T FEAR THE DEVIL ANYMORE

There was a time in my life when I used to be afraid of the devil. Occasionally I would picture in my mind's eye God and His heavenly host battling a celestial war against the devil and his demons somewhere in outer space. The eternal struggle between Good and Evil, if you will. But that was before I was saved and began studying the Scriptures, specifically meditating on key verses like those found in the twentieth chapter of Revelation.

The book of Revelation provides us with an unclouded glimpse at precisely who this disgraced angel is and the defined boundaries of his authority. Have you ever read that incredible Bible passage where the devil gets picked up and thrown into the abyss before the thousand-year millennial reign of Jesus Christ? God and Satan must have been battling each other for a long time before the Lord finally got the upper hand in that scuffle, right? Not hardly. In fact, God isn't even the one who throws Satan into the abyss. It is one lone angel who accomplishes that feat. Just one angel holding "the key of the abyss and a great chain in his hand."[171] That's it. One angel.

It won't even be much of a struggle, for we're then told, "And he laid hold of the dragon, the serpent of old, who is the devil and Satan, and bound him for a thousand years; and he threw him into the abyss, and shut it and sealed it over him."[172]

No, the devil isn't all that powerful, really. He is a demonic deceiver who has duped millions and millions of

---

171 Revelation 20:1
172 Revelation 20:2-3

people into crediting more to him than is necessary. So let us not be guilty of doing that any longer.

It is for reasons such as this that Scripture exhorts us to "Fear God, and give Him glory,"[173] but only to "Resist the devil and he will flee from you."[174] We are to fear God and resist the devil. That's a massive difference.

Satan is a coward and, with his tail tucked between his legs, runs away when you resist him by God's grace. Fearing God, on the other hand, is so much more than merely a reverential fear. If God expected only to be revered by us, then He would have said so. After all, it's not reverence that makes one wise but "the fear of the LORD is the beginning of wisdom."[175]

WHY THIS ALL MATTERS

I'm highlighting some of these eternal truths so that you'll understand that God is actually the One in total control over all things and at all times. There is no power struggle in the heavens, nor is there a tug-of-war going on within the Trinity, either.

God alone is the Divine Power pulling all the strings in this universe. And that includes even the strings we are not comfortable with. If something seems off-color with regards to the severe persecution of Christian people, then we should look no further than God's throne. Never does God author sin and He "will not allow you to be tempted beyond what you are able, but with the temptation will provide the way of escape also, so that you will be able to

---

173 Revelation 14:7
174 James 4:7
175 Proverbs 9:10

endure it."[176] Yet the buck of responsibility always stops at the feet of the Almighty.

So don't ever lose sight of who is sitting on the throne and, consequently, gets to decide what commandments we must obey.

THE PROBLEM WITH PARTIAL OBEDIENCE

God didn't send His Son to die on a cross in order to save only a few thousand people in one Jewish city, then sit back and wait hundreds of years for billions of people to die and perish in Hell. Certainly not! The apostle Peter warned his readers that "it is time for judgment to begin with the household of God; and if it begins with us first, what will be the outcome for those who do not obey the gospel of God?"[177] God's plan for the redeemed—determined in eternity past—has always been for us to glorify Him while sharing the faith that is in us with those around us.

And yet, when a child chooses to remain defiant to his father's will, the rod will not go unused.

Tertullian, the second century Christian author, is credited for having first said, "The blood of the martyrs is the seed of the Church."[178] It reminds me of how the persecution of true Christians will always suit God's plan. We may not prefer God's usage of pain and suffering, but it certainly accomplishes the result He intends.

Pastor and author Charles Swindoll wrote, "A loving God using pain to produce good in His children may

---

176 1 Corinthians 10:13

177 1 Peter 4:17

178 Wikipedia.org, www.httpen.wikipedia.org/wiki/Apologeticus (accessed January 4, 2013).

sound harsh, until you consider that the most loving thing He ever did was also the most painful—putting His only Son on the cross."[179]

Partial obedience to His revealed will is not what the Lord intended for His people, neither in biblical times nor in today's Christianity. As we'll see in more detail in the next chapter, the Lord Himself unleashed religious persecution against the believers in Jerusalem in order that the redeemed might be scattered into Judea and Samaria with the gospel. It was only after the church forsook the comfortable confines of Jerusalem's walls—in exchange for being wholly obedient to Christ's command—that God then holstered the prodding stick of religious persecution.

Understanding—and heeding—this warning applies to every believer today as well. It would be unwise to tempt the Lord any further in this regard. That is not God's will for your life today.

WHAT TO DO ABOUT AGAG

Yet before we dive into the terribly fascinating topic of religious persecution found in the book of Acts, it may prove beneficial to first take a stroll down memory lane to an incident earlier in Israel's history. This sobering reminder will set the stage for the substance of Divine Persecution found in the next chapter.

What we each need to beware of is having an attitude of, "Oh well, God will just have to forgive me if I don't share the gospel." Chastening always begins with God's children first. We need to understand that there are stern

179 Charles Swindoll, God's Masterwork, Volume Five: 2 Thessalonians Through Revelation (The Lockman Foundation, 1998), page 57.

consequences to both our wicked actions and our sinful omissions.

I want us to consider the severe penalty to King Saul's lack of being *wholly* obedient to the mission God gave him. After all, God expects His people to be much more than merely 99% obedient to His commands, right?

Ultimately, we need to understand what King Saul was forced to learn the hard way. We need to realize that there are permanent and potentially life-altering consequences for stopping short of hacking Agag to pieces.

A CLEAR PLAN OF ANNIHILATION

In 1 Samuel 15, God sent Samuel the prophet to inform King Saul that the Israelites were to go to war against the Amalakites. God wanted the Israelites to completely annihilate the Amalakites from the face of the planet. They weren't allowed to leave even one animal alive, let alone an Amalakite man, woman, or child.

The LORD's mission was crystal-clear. King Saul should have been wholly obedient to the command. Sadly, Saul chose to disobey God in the finer details of his mission, wrongly assuming that God would be satisfied with *partial* obedience.

He was dead wrong, however, and that one act of rebellion cost him both the crown and his life.

The LORD God gave King Saul a clear and unique mission. God planned to impose final judgment against the Amalakites because they had attacked Israel in the wilderness after He delivered them from Egyptian slavery.[180] God

---

180 c.f. Exodus 17:8–16

had decided to put to death both man and woman, child and infant, ox and sheep, camel and donkey. In other words, He had chosen to utterly destroy anything that breathed and was linked to Amalek. All memory of Amalek was to be wiped off the face of the planet.

WATCH YOUR MOUTH

Be careful what you say or think about the integrity of God's edict. King Saul should have been wholly obedient to the command of the LORD. Unfortunately, Israel's king fashioned a standard of convenient obedience that suited his own agenda rather than God's. As the prophetic mouthpiece for the LORD, Samuel concluded that such partial obedience "is as iniquity and idolatry."[181]

One of the things that strikes me about this passage is that God considers anything less than 100% obedience as iniquity and idolatry. Christian obedience that progresses no further than what is convenient for the moment is considered iniquitous and idolatrous as far as God is concerned.

Question: What do you think about that? *Iniquity. Idolatry.* It seems that God is downright serious about this whole obedience thing. God's revealed will regarding obedience to His Word is pretty clear.

In 1 Samuel 15:7, King Saul and the Israelites went to war and defeated the Amalakites with relative ease, chasing them throughout much of the Amalakite territory. So far, so good. When the Lord provides a mission

---

181 1 Samuel 15:23

to His people, He ensures its success, so long as we remain faithful to our calling.

Unfortunately for King Saul and the Israelites, the sin of covetousness set in, and as a nation, they reaped the consequences of that sin for many generations thereafter.

THE PROBLEM WITH COVETOUSNESS

Being set aflame by the lust of the flesh, the Israelite people fixed their gaze on the booty of plunder and turned their hearts from following the trail of obedient compliance. They did well to kill most of the Amalakite people with the edge of the sword, but in their spiritual rebellion, they also spared Agag, the Amalakite king, and the choice livestock.

Verse nine reads, "But Saul and the people spared Agag and the best of the sheep, the oxen, the fatlings, the lambs, and all that was good, and were not willing to destroy them utterly; but everything despised and worthless, that they utterly destroyed."

Saul failed miserably in his God-given mission. He was mostly obedient, but according to God's exacting standard, mostly obedient is the twin of total failure. Both he and the Israelites were not wholly devoted to the mission God had given them to fulfill.

Saul and the Israelites were willing to be obedient to the LORD God's commission, but only to the point that it suited their comfort level. Greed and the lust for riches had turned their hearts far from worshiping God. All that the LORD considered worthless, detestable, and which should have been utterly destroyed, the Israelites considered good and were unwilling to destroy. Such is the rationalism of a disobedient heart bent toward the sin of self-gratification.

Partial obedience to the revealed will of a holy God is idolatry at its very core.

Did you catch that? Be sure that you understand this critical truth.

A BLAME-SHIFTING KING

The word of the LORD then came to Samuel because of King Saul's misbehavior, and so the prophet was commissioned to proclaim divine judgment against Saul's partial obedience. Notice the wickedness that dripped from Saul's lips in verse thirteen, "I have carried out the command of the LORD." Samuel challenged that lie by pointing to the overwhelming amount of evidence to the contrary, referring to the Amalakite livestock being held back from annihilation. Not unlike Adam and Eve in the Garden of Eden, King Saul shifted the blame for his sin onto his fellow Israelites, saying, "They have brought them from the Amalakites, for the people spared the best of the sheep and oxen to sacrifice to the LORD your God; but the rest we have utterly destroyed."[182]

Stop right there for a moment. Don't we sometimes do this as well? Too often I'm quick to blame others—or even my circumstances—before ever pointing the finger at the person staring back in the mirror. There is always an excuse for our disobedience. Always a circumstance in which to shift blame.

---

182 1 Samuel 15:15

IT'S ALL OR NOTHING TO GOD

God's prophet then pronounced the penalty for King Saul's sin. The punishment was severe, but it was also just. Scripture is clear about the righteousness of God's decrees when it says of Him, "So that You are justified when You speak and blameless when You judge."[183] When it came to Saul's disobedience (aka: partial obedience), no one benefited in the end. Not even Agag.

In verse eighteen, Samuel reminded Saul that "the LORD sent you on a mission," and then in verse nineteen that Saul did "not obey the voice of the LORD, but rushed upon the spoil and did what was evil in the sight of the LORD." Notice that Samuel does not commend Saul for his partial obedience, but rather pronounces it as evil in the sight of the LORD.

Fellow Christians, do not presume that God is satisfied with even a 99% effort toward obedience on our part when it comes to obeying the commands of His revealed will. He requires radical, unwavering allegiance to the mission in which we are called. It's not always easy, but it is always our responsibility. To be disobedient to the Lord's commandments is sin. To be disobedient to the Lord's revealed will of Great Commission Discipleship is, therefore, as iniquity and idolatry.

THE PROBLEM WITH TRYING TO BRIBE GOD

Still justifying himself in verses twenty and twenty-one, King Saul said,

---

183 Psalm 51:4

> "I did obey the voice of the LORD, and went on the mission in which the LORD sent me, and have brought back Agag the king of Amalek, and have utterly destroyed the Amalakites. But the people took some of the spoil, sheep and oxen, the choicest of the things devoted to destruction, to sacrifice to the LORD your God at Gilgal."

Observe first, that an impenitent conscience will attempt to justify a lack of faithfulness to God rather than openly confess it. Second, Saul admits he knew what God commanded, but that his obedience fell short of the divine requirement. Third, the sinfulness of partial obedience attempts to bribe God by sacrificing to Him detestable things devoted to destruction.

I believe I'm justified in saying that God was not amused.

Samuel then rebuked the disobedient king, saying, "Has the LORD as much delight in burnt offerings and sacrifices as in obeying the voice of the LORD? Behold, to obey is better than sacrifice, and to heed than the fat of rams."[184] In other words, God is interested in people who are radically and wholly obedient to Him, rather than obedient only to the point that it is convenient. Such convenient obedience, Samuel declared, is rebellion, the sin of divination, insubordination, idolatry, and a rejection of God's Word.

Rebellion. Divination. Insubordination. Idolatry. Rejection.

Are you at all feeling uncomfortable about your level of obedience to God's revealed will? God is by no means impressed with our half-hearted efforts at obeying His Great Commission mandate.

---

184 1 Samuel 15:22

REJECTING THE WORD OF GOD

Convicted by his guilt-ridden conscience, Saul finally admitted to his cosmic treason and confessed, "I have sinned; I have indeed transgressed the command of the LORD and your words because I feared the people and listened to their voice."[185] There it is, plain and simple. To be even partially obedient to God's Word and to cease at that point is sin and a transgression of the commandment of God. For King Saul, unfortunately, it was too late. The sands in the hourglass of God's patience had run out. The LORD's judgment against Saul's insubordination and idolatry was that the kingdom of Israel was being torn from his grasp—permanently. God had rejected him from being king over Israel and was preparing to give it to a young shepherd named David.

The Lord gives and the Lord alone takes away. Don't ever forget this precious truth.

All this divine judgment was the direct result of King Saul not being wholly obedient to the mission God had given him. He was mostly obedient, yes—but being mostly obedient to the commands of Almighty God is nowhere close to the minimum requirement. As God's prophet declared, Saul had "rejected the word of the LORD," and he paid dearly because of it.[186]

CAN I BORROW YOUR SWORD?

It would be a terrible injustice not to pause for a moment and take notice of how Samuel worshipped the Lord after all these events. Samuel's radical faithfulness serves as a

---

185 1 Samuel 15:24
186 1 Samuel 15:26

glaring beam of light in contrast to the shadow of Saul's dark rebellion. The comparison is rather graphic to say the least, but also quite beautiful.

To be an Old Testament prophet of the Lord is not an office I would have envied. That was a tough ministry. It seems the prophets were always delivering grave news and the recipients rarely wanted to hear what God's man had to say. In fact, most people probably pulled their shutters closed whenever a legitimate prophet of the Lord strolled into town. If the prophet wasn't delivering grim news for a particular sinner, it usually meant the city itself was going up in flames soon.

No, when a legitimate prophet of the LORD God wanted to meet with you, it wasn't often that he was stopping by for biscuits and tea. And Agag should have known that.

Once Samuel accompanied King Saul back to the place of worship (so that Saul could save face before the elders and the people of Israel), Samuel then returned to deal with yet another wicked king. Upon his return, Samuel said, "Bring me Agag, the king of the Amalakites."[187]

I assume Samuel was a bit flustered that day, having to deal with two wicked kings back-to-back. He had already delivered a harsh condemnation to Israel's king, and now he was planning a radical act of worship at the expense of one of Israel's all-time enemies.

One thing worthy of notice from this passage is that just because a person neglects his or her appointed ministry, that doesn't make it acceptable for the rest of us to allow the duty to go unfulfilled altogether. Samuel knew this all

---

187 1 Samuel 15:32

too well, and so he summoned the Amalakite king in order to finish what Saul had left undone.

Agag presumed he'd escaped the sentence of death, for he entered Samuel's presence cheerfully, saying, "Surely the bitterness of death is past."[188] On the contrary, however, the moment of Divine Judgment had finally arrived. Answering Agag's foolish presumption, Samuel replied, "As your sword has made women childless, so shall your mother be childless among women."[189]

And with that brief exchange, Samuel began to worship the LORD his God.

TO HACK IS BETTER THAN SACRIFICE

With a sword in hand, the prophet rushed upon Agag, and "Samuel hewed Agag to pieces *before the LORD* at Gilgal" (emphasis mine). The text is bloody, graphic, and violent. But there's also a sense of goodness to it, because divine justice was finally being served. At last, someone was being wholly obedient to the revealed will of Almighty God.

Notice the words, "before the LORD." As Samuel was hacking Agag's flesh to pieces, he was worshipping God!

Do not miss this!

As the prophet of the Lord severed each body part and the Amalakite's blood soaked into the ground, Samuel worshipped God. This is a tremendously explicit passage of Scripture, yet it potently describes how God expects to be worshipped during every facet of life. Even when doing so is uncomfortable, inconvenient, or downright nasty.

---

188 *Ibid.*
189 1 Samuel 15:33

As Samuel's sword rained down over and over again, the LORD God was worshipped. Not through the violence or even in the death of one of His creatures, but in the fact that Samuel cared enough to carry out the finer details of God's command to King Saul.

This is vitally important and has tremendous relevance for us—even today—regarding God's revealed will for Great Commission Discipleship.

TOOLS DON'T TALK BACK
TO THE CRAFTSMAN

We American Christians would do well to meditate often upon the attitudes and actions of both King Saul and Samuel the prophet. God has given each of us today a mission to proclaim the gospel to every soul on Earth—both to saved and unsaved people. Even to an Amalakite, if you could find one.

We have not been commissioned to slay the enemy, but to love our enemies. We are not allowed to hate our enemies, but to loathe the sin that enslaves them. Our mission is not to hack sinners to pieces, but—by God's grace—to purge unbelief from around the world.

God is dishonored when we don't obey His commands with relentless and unwavering allegiance. But there is always someone else the Lord can use if we prove negligent in our assigned ministry. He has many hammers to choose from, after all.

The Lord can raise up children of Abraham from stones, and "the eyes of the LORD move to and fro throughout the earth that He may strongly support those whose heart is completely His."[190] If we choose not to honor God by being obedient to His revealed will of Great Commission Discipleship, He will be dishonored and we'll reap the consequence. Nevertheless, the Lord will not allow His plan to be thwarted. He will appoint another to succeed where you or I have committed the rebellious sin of omission.

As one New Testament writer penned, "Therefore, to one who knows the right thing to do and does not do it, to him it is sin."[191]

GOD DOESN'T LIKE PLAYING SECOND FIDDLE

The Lord is sovereign. His plans will never be frustrated.

Remember Joseph? Joseph responded to the treachery of his wicked brothers by saying, "You meant evil against me, *but God meant it for good* in order to bring about this present result" (emphasis mine).[192]

When God delivered Israel during the time Deborah judged them, the opportunity for national glory was given into the hands of Barak, the commander of Israel's army.[193] Barak flinched, however, wanting to place conditions on the extent of his obedience. He said to Deborah, "If you will go with me, then I will go; but if you will not go with me, I will not go."[194] Rebuking his cowardice, Deborah replied, "I will surely go with you; nevertheless, the honor shall not be yours on the journey that you are about to take, for the LORD will sell Sisera into the hands of a

---

190 2 Chronicles 16:9
191 James 4:17
192 Genesis 50:20
193 See Judges 4–5
194 Judges 4:8

woman."[195] That woman ended up being Jael, who drove a tent peg through the side of Sisera's head.

God accomplished His sovereign plan despite the immoral actions of Joseph's kin. God accomplished His sovereign plan despite Barak's military lunacy. And God accomplished His sovereign plan without King Saul's faithfulness, as well. That is something you and I need to remember today. God does not need us, but He wants to use us. The Lord's plans will never be spoiled due to the negligent frailty of sinful men and women, even if they are His beloved children. There is always another who will step up to the plate and be wholly consecrated to perform all the Lord's work.

Question: Is that someone you? Are you willing to be radically and wholly consecrated to the Lord, performing all He commands you to do? Are you really interested in knowing and performing God's will for your life, or are you having second thoughts right about now?

For Such a Time as This

In the book of Esther, we read about one of the Amalakite's descendants (due to King Saul's disobedience in 1 Samuel 15, incidentally) named Haman, the son of Hammedatha the Agagite. Haman became a thorn in Israel's side, concocting a murderous plan to annihilate every Jew once and for all. If not for the sovereign, covenant love that God has for His people, Haman no doubt would have succeeded.

When the fateful decree was issued that the lives and property of the Jews were free game to any and all,

---

195 Judges 4:9

Esther's older cousin, Mordecai, heard about it and covered himself in sackcloth, crying out to the Lord. Sending word to Queen Esther, he said,

> "Do not imagine that you in the king's palace can escape any more than all the Jews. For if you remain silent at this time, relief and deliverance will arise for the Jews from *another place* and you and your father's house will perish. And who knows whether you have not attained royalty *for such a time as this*?" (emphasis mine)[196]

What about you? Has God placed you where you are for such a time as this? God will certainly bring about all His plans to fruition, but woe to that person who puts the patience of the Lord to the test.

I appreciate very much what J.C. Ryle had to say about the worthlessness of a shallow religion. He wrote, "There is a common, worldly kind of Christianity in this day, which many have, and think they have enough—a cheap Christianity which offends nobody, and requires no sacrifice—which costs nothing, and is worth nothing."[197]

Frankly, a religion worth anything is a religion that is worth everything. If Christ means anything at all to us, He should mean absolutely everything to us.

Don't you agree?

---

196 Esther 4:13–14
197 Mark Dever, <u>The Gospel & Personal Evangelism</u> (Crossway Books, 2007), page 42; J.C. Ryle, <u>Holiness</u> (1883; repr., Grand Rapids, MI: Baker, 1979), 204.

BUT WHAT DOES A HEADLESS KING
HAVE TO DO WITH GOD'S WILL?

The Lord's displeasure over King Saul's disobedience should serve as a loud, stinging reminder to each and every Christian today. This author included.

As believers in the post-Resurrection era, we have each been issued a divine mission to go, share the gospel with every creature, and to make disciples of all the nations. To not be wholly obedient to this command is sin, and all sin has its consequence.

"Do not be deceived," the Scripture warns, "God is not mocked; for whatever a man sows, this he will also reap."[198] If we, who call on the name of the Lord, continue to sow laziness in our personal devotions, cherish lukewarm pews of convenience rather than dying daily, or lack zeal in our love for both the saved and the unsaved, then we may reap divine judgment sooner rather than later.

Please notice, however, that although God immediately pronounced judgment against King Saul, He withheld His omnipotent hand until a later date. Saul remained king over Israel and lived many years after his failure with the Amalakites.

Could it be that perhaps the Lord was granting Saul an opportunity to repent and return with faithful obedience? After all, the Lord waited nearly two full years for the early church to leave Jerusalem before He allowed them to be persecuted in Acts chapter eight. Could God also be holding back His judgment against any one of us at this very moment? Could He be waiting for us to finish (or

---

198 Galatians 6:7

even begin?) the ministry we've been appointed to, rather than making excuses for our lack of effort?

I wonder.

WHO KILLED KING SAUL?

Regardless, however, do not misinterpret the fact that it was God—not man or devil—who ultimately killed King Saul. A Philistine archer launched the arrow that pierced his flesh, and Saul subsequently committed suicide when he "took his sword and fell on it."[199] But God in His sovereignty ordained all of it to be. As it clearly states in 1 Chronicles 10:13-14,

> "So Saul died for his treason which he committed against the LORD, because of the word of the LORD which he did not keep; and also because he asked counsel of a medium, making inquiry of it, and did not inquire of the LORD. *Therefore He killed him* and turned the kingdom to David the son of Jesse" (emphasis mine).

The consequence of Saul's idolatrous disobedience stands as a warning to everyone today who names the name of Christ. As sheep prone to wander, we each need to be reminded of how important it is to be passionate about our own personal discipleship, following through with our Lord's command to go and make disciples.

The requirement for total obedience is as potent today as it was to the early church in the book of Acts. In the same way that there was a severe consequence for the early

---

199 1 Samuel 31:3, 4

church being only partially obedient to God's revealed will of Great Commission Discipleship, there will be a consequence for us as well—whether in this life or at the Judgment Seat of Christ.

Beloved, be intentionally radical about your love for Jesus Christ. This is most certainly God's will for your life today.

IF YOU'RE BREATHING, YOU HAVE ANOTHER CHANCE

President Abraham Lincoln wrote a letter on October 4, 1864, from his office in Washington, D.C. The letter is not exactly famous, but it certainly is interesting.

It reads as follows:

> Upon condition that Roswell McIntyre of Co. E, Sixth Regiment of New York Calvary, returns to his regiment and faithfully serves out his time, or until lawfully discharged, he is fully pardoned for any supposed desertion heretofore committed; this paper is his pass to his regiment.[200]

What is so fascinating about this particular letter is that on the bottom left corner was scribbled: "Taken from the body of R. McIntyre at the battle of Five Forks, Va., 1865."

Roswell McIntyre was a Union solider who, in a moment of cowardice, deserted his military post and went AWOL. He was eventually captured and imprisoned, but President Lincoln gave him a second chance to reclaim his dignity. The choice was the soldier's alone to make. To his credit,

---

200 MoreIllustrations.com, www.moreillustrations.com/Illustrations/faithfulness%201.html (accessed January 4, 2013).

Mr. McIntyre chose to take Lincoln up on that promise and rejoined his troop. A year later, that decision cost him his life. Instead of living out the remainder of his years as an imprisoned and disgraced coward, he died a brave and heroic soldier at the battle of Five Forks in Virginia.

So is every Christian who obediently engages in the very next opportunity of ministry that crosses his or her path. Past failures should not dictate our future obedience. The Father of our Lord Jesus Christ remains the ever-living God of second chances.

BE WHOLLY DEVOTED TO GOD

When King Solomon arose from before the altar of the Lord, he addressed the assembly of Israel with a loud voice, saying, "Let your heart therefore by *wholly* devoted to the LORD our God, to walk in His statutes, and to keep His commandments" (emphasis mine).[201]

May that be the case with every one of God's children as we obey His revealed will, making disciples of Jesus Christ for the glory of God alone.

---

201 1 Kings 8:61

CHAPTER TEN

GOD'S WILL DOES NOT INVOLVE COMPLACENT FAITH

"Therefore, to one who knows the right thing to do and does not do it, to him it is sin." (James 4:17)

"If a church is effective in accomplishing its mission, it will be reaching lost people. If a church is not reaching nonbelievers, then it is not being successful—no matter how well it may be doing in terms of increases in attendance, donations, and facilities." —James Emery White

OUR EXALTED SAVIOR guards the purity of His people with a holy passion. Just ask Ananias and Sapphira, who were both struck dead after donating a large chunk of money for the needs of the poor because they lied about the finer details of the gift. God is serious about the sin of lying. But He is also serious about the sin of spiritual complacency. When God issues a command, each person must decide for himself or herself whether to respond like young Samuel and say, "Speak, for Your servant is listening," or just take a page out of Jonah's book and board the first ship to Tarshish.[202]

TO OBEY OR NOT TO OBEY

In Acts 1:8, Jesus issued the last instructions of His Great Commission mandate with a three-fold geographic progression, saying, "And you shall be My witnesses both in Jerusalem, and in all Judea and Samaria, and even to the remotest part of the earth." In fact, the entire book of Acts can be outlined with these three geographic destinations in mind.[203]

It was in this progression of geography that the early church missed the mark of God's revealed will and, subsequently, suffered the penalty of it.

Our Lord expected the disciples to commence with the proclamation of His gospel first in Jerusalem, then to Judea and Samaria, and finally to the remotest part of the earth. The problem with those early believers, however, was that they simply never got around to leaving the comfortable city of Jerusalem. Once the day of Pentecost had come and gone, the church remained in Jerusalem for close to two full years before being thrown out by God Himself. The church had become complacent in their partial obedience, refusing to leave the convenience of Jerusalem for the fertile crops of the Judean mission field.

---

202 1 Samuel 3:10
203 "Jerusalem" in 1:9–8:3; "Judea and Samaria" in 8:4–12:25; and "the remotest part of the earth" in 13:1–28:31

Do We Have a Problem Here?

Essentially, the main problem in chapters 1-7 in the book of Acts was this: *The gospel of Jesus Christ never traveled beyond the walls of Jerusalem.* This was a significant obstacle to God's revealed will of Great Commission Discipleship. After all, how can you fulfill the Great Commission to all the nations if every Christian refuses to leave the very first city? The Jewish disciples were huddled together in a cozy Christianity, keeping the good news all to themselves within Jerusalem's walls. They were unwilling to venture out into Judea and Samaria and beyond with the saving gospel.

But why would they do such a thing?

There Is Nothing New Under the Sun

For one reason or another, those early believers chose not to be fully compliant to Christ's revealed will. Like King Saul, they were satisfied with partial obedience rather than remaining true to their core mission. But I'm personally finding it difficult to really blame them all that much. After all, the Lord was saving souls by the thousands seemingly each time Peter or John opened their mouths to preach, so it may have never dawned on them to fully pursue the mission they were given, rather than sit still.

No, I don't blame the early church one bit. But that's only because I'm certain I would have been doing the exact same thing.

Those Hellenist Jews, who traveled many miles away from their homes in order to celebrate Pentecost, who heard the gospel, believed it and were saved, for the most part remained in Jerusalem.[204] They didn't return back to their own cities and homes. There weren't any Christian churches back in their own towns and villages, so they were quite content to sojourn in Jerusalem where all the excitement was.

This isn't too difficult to understand when we read, "Everyone kept feeling a sense of awe; and many wonders and signs were taking place through the apostles."[205] When one stops to consider that the daily fellowship was so wonderfully sweet, and that they "were taking their meals together with gladness and sincerity of heart, praising God and having favor with all the people," it's no wonder the 5,000+ redeemed weren't hurrying to get back to the humdrum of their old Jewish lives.[206] Add to that the fact that "the Lord was adding to their number day by day those who were being saved," and I can find almost no fault with them myself.[207]

But again, that's only because I'm a sinner who—like them—typically prefers the comforts of Christian fellowship rather than the lonely trail of evangelistic enterprise.

Nevertheless, as wonderful as all that must have been there in Jerusalem, it wasn't God's long-term plan for Great Commission Discipleship. Jerusalem was not to be the Christian hub where believers congregated until the Lord's second coming.

---

204 i.e. "Parthians and Medes and Elamites, and residents of Mesopotamia, Judea and Cappadocia, Pontus and Asia, Phyrgia and Pamphylia, Egypt and the districts of Libya around Cyrene, and visitors from Rome, both Jews and proselytes, Cretans and Arabs" (Acts 2:9-11).
205 Acts 2:43
206 Acts 5:46-47
207 Acts 5:47

Jerusalem was the starting line for Christian disciple-ship—not the finish line.

WHEN GOD PLAYS TRUTH OR DARE

The Lord—who is sovereign over all things—permitted the believers in Jerusalem to be persecuted so that they would begin scattering the gospel seed around Judea and Samaria. Once the gospel was being proclaimed in Samaria and its vicinity, the Lord withdrew His prodding stick. However, we shouldn't move on to the failure of the early church's partial obedience until we first highlight the extent of their loyalty.

It's only fair to do so.

Although the early believers weren't being wholly obe-dient to Jesus Christ's revealed plan for Great Commission Discipleship, God was absolutely blessing the faithfulness that was present. And there was plenty of radical obedience to bless, after all.

God is a mercifully compassionate Father who is faithful to bless those who bless Him. But there's also a limit to God's patience in that He cannot disregard the fact that His chil-dren simply ignored the latter details of His Commission, choosing instead to sojourn in a Christianity of conve-nience. Therefore, in spite of the abundant blessings and the thousands of Jews being saved there in Jerusalem, God chose to scatter the church into all the nations by unleashing the beast of religious persecution.

Sometimes you have to set the church pews ablaze just to get the Christians to exit the building!

MIND OVER MATTER: GOD
MINDS AND SO IT MATTERS

Aren't you glad we serve a God who controls every aspect of this universe we call home? He has a lot more than just the whole world in His hands.

He cherishes and collects the prayers of every saint and grieves alongside us during our struggles and trials.

Remember Job? After God allowed Job to vent his frustrations over life's calamities, He answered that godly man with essentially, "Just trust Me." God knows what we need. He seeks our ultimate good, and if we will but trust Him—walking by faith and not by sight—He never fails to take notice.

God is sovereign, even in the pain and suffering of genuine Christians. He must be, or He can't be God.

It is for this very reason that James, the half-brother of Jesus, exhorted his persecuted readers to "Consider it all joy, my brethren, when you encounter various trials, knowing that the testing of your faith produces endurance."[208] It's also the reason why the apostle Peter could write, "In this you greatly rejoice, even though now for a little while, if necessary, you have been distressed by various trials, so that the truth of your faith, being more precious than gold which is perishable, even though tested by fire, may be found to result in praise and glory and honor at the revelation of Jesus Christ."[209]

Persecution will always manifest the perseverance of

---

208 James 1:2-3
209 1 Peter 1:6-7

genuine faith, and such faith inevitably results in the praise and glory of our God and Savior Jesus Christ.

THE DEVIL NEEDS PERMISSION

When Satan asked God for permission to test Job by killing his children and harming his body, the Lord permitted it. God had His reasons. Satan can't even lift a finger against us without God's permission. I don't know about you, but this bewildering truth gives me great comfort. Yet alongside this marvelous assurance comes the knowledge that when trials, tests, and persecutions enter into our midst, none of that escapes the Lord's permission either.

Understanding this biblical truth is essential for coming to grips with why God allowed Christians to be brutally persecuted, both in the book of Acts and throughout the many centuries since.

But for us to truly understand why God allowed the early church to be persecuted in order to motivate them toward obedience, it's necessary to take a jet tour through the first eleven chapters of the book of Acts.

So here we go.

THIS IS A "NO STANDING" ZONE

Immediately after Jesus issued the final details of His revealed Great Commission mandate, the miraculous Ascension took place. Jesus was lifted up while they were looking on, and a cloud received Him out of their sight. As the disciples were "gazing intently into the sky," two angels emerged in their midst, appearing as "men in white clothing."[210]

---

210 Acts 1:10

What these two angels said simply fascinates me. God could have had those angelic messengers say any number of things, yet their very first words were, "Men of Galilee, why do you stand looking into the sky?"[211]

This seems like a bizarre question, particularly because Jesus was floating through the clouds right before their eyes! Yet then again, it isn't so strange when we consider what the disciples were supposed to be doing at that very moment.

They were supposed to be boarding the first chariot to Jerusalem!

The angels then say, in verse eleven, that Jesus "will come in just the same way as you have watched Him go into heaven," but it seems strange to insert a doctrinal teaching regarding the Second Coming in such an obscure passage. Furthermore, it is unlikely the Lord would use two unidentified angels to explain—with such brevity even—about the manner in which Jesus will return one day. God would soon enough use the apostle Paul to pen inspired epistles detailing that rapturous event.[212]

Although the angels' pronouncement regarding Christ's inevitable return would have certainly been encouraging, I believe the real issue lies in their first question: "Men of Galilee, why do you stand looking into the sky?"

GET YOUR HEAD OUT OF THE CLOUDS

What we have here is a mild reprimand. The disciples needed to recognize the importance of obedience according to God's timeline, not theirs. They should've been sprinting down "the mount called Olivet, which is near Jerusalem, a

---

211 Acts 1:11
212 e.g. 1 and 2 Thessalonians

Sabbath day's journey away," but they just stood there with their eyes fixed on clouds.[213]

To put the angels' announcement in the context of today's vernacular, they were essentially saying, "Get your heads out of the clouds and get moving! There is no dilly-dallying when the Son of God gives you a mission. To Jerusalem, and fast! Jesus will certainly return, but you need to focus on what you have been commanded to do today."

And what does the Scripture say immediately happened following the angel's words? Acts 1:12 tells us, saying, "Then they returned to Jerusalem from the Mount of Olives."

God sent His disciples two angelic messengers to remind them that He is serious about this Great Commission business. This is important stuff—determined by God before the foundation of the world—and they weren't permitted to go about it flippantly. Immediate and absolute allegiance, faithfulness, and deliberate obedience to Jesus Christ were the ingredients required.

It is what's required still today, by the way. This is God's revealed will for every man, woman, and child who names the name of Christ.

Really, these brief verses set the stage for the remainder of not only the book of Acts, but our mission today as well. God is saying to each of us today, "Hey, Christians, get your heads out of the clouds and start making disciples!"

WHY BUY THE COW WHEN THE MILK IS FREE?

The New Testament church was born when the Day of Pentecost had come.

---

213 Acts 1:12

Pentecost is one of three national feasts in which all Jews were required to leave their homes and travel to Jerusalem in order to celebrate. Pentecost (which means "fiftieth") refers to the Feast of Harvest or Feast of Weeks, and was celebrated in Jerusalem fifty days after Passover.[214] Seeing as it was a Feast of Harvest, Leviticus 23:20 commanded an offering of first fruits to be presented. So when the Holy Spirit descended that day in Jerusalem, it signified that those disciples were the first fruits of the Lord's harvest of all believers to come.

It was under these amazing and festive circumstances that God unrolled His revealed blueprint for Great Commission Discipleship.

When God Plants a Church

Pentecost takes place fifty days after Passover. Upon the Lord's resurrection, Scripture tells us that Jesus provided "many convincing proofs, appearing to them over a period of forty days."[215] Jesus commanded the disciples "to stay in the city until you are clothed with power from on high."[216] Therefore, when the disciples were gathered in the upper room during Pentecost, they had been waiting ten days before being miraculously clothed with heavenly raiment.

God has impeccable timing. He is never delinquent in fulfilling His promises.

As just mentioned in Luke 24:49, Jesus told the disciples

---

214 c.f. Leviticus 23:16 and Exodus 34:22-23
215 Acts 1:3
216 Luke 24:49

"to stay in the city *until* you are clothed with power from on high" (emphasis mine).

Notice the word "until."

Obviously, once the Holy Spirit had appeared in Jerusalem, they were free—literally commanded—to then begin moving on to phase two of the Great Commission's *geographic* progression. The next step for the church was to begin taking the gospel into Judea and Samaria. As previously mentioned, there was at least a two-year period of time between Jesus being raised from the dead and Stephen being martyred at the end of Acts chapter seven. Therefore, the Lord had been quite patient with the church there in the city of Jerusalem.

Once the disciples had received the Holy Spirit, Peter preached a mighty sermon, during which the Lord saved about 3,000 souls. The believers then obediently spread the gospel around the city, living godly lives that both honored and glorified the Lord. As the church committed itself to radical worship, and the apostles were faithful to their preaching ministries, "the Lord was adding to their number day by day those who were being saved."[217]

Take a fresh look at all that was happening during that time and maybe you'll appreciate why those Hellenistic Jews weren't so eager to leave Jerusalem and go back home, many hundreds of miles away, where there were no other churches or fellow believers.

> "They were continually devoting themselves to the apostles' teaching and to fellowship, to the breaking of bread and to prayer. Everyone kept feeling a sense of

---

217 Acts 2:47

awe; and many wonders and signs were taking place
through the apostles. And all those who had believed
were together and had all things in common; and
they began selling their property and possessions and
were sharing them with all, as anyone might have
need. Day by day continuing with one mind in the
temple, and breaking bread from house to house,
they were taking their meals together with gladness
and sincerity of heart, praising God and having favor
with all the people. And the Lord was adding to their
number day by day those who were being saved."[218]

TOO MANY MOUTHS TO FEED

In Acts chapter three, a lame man got healed, and after
Peter preached another sermon, hundreds more got saved.
It says in Acts 4:4, "But many of those who had heard the
message believed; and the number of the men came to be
about five thousand."

The Lord was building the church at a rapid pace there
in Jerusalem. Only men were numbered in those days,
so when you take into consideration their wives and any
children with them, the total number at this point could
have been well over 20,000 people.

That's not a church. It's a city!

The church was certainly growing by leaps and bounds,
but only in Jerusalem. This would quickly become a *good*
problem for everyone around Judea and Samaria.

Overpopulation became a massive issue to be addressed.
Expecting to be in Jerusalem only a few days, the thousands of visiting Hellenist Jews who got saved during the

---

218 Acts 2:42-47

celebration of Pentecost didn't bring enough money to support their families' long-term needs. Most didn't have homes in Jerusalem to live in permanently.

Notice what it says in Acts 4:32-35:

> "And the congregation of those who believed were of one heart and soul; and not one of them claimed that anything belonging to him was his own, but all things were common property to them. And with great power the apostles were giving testimony to the resurrection of the Lord Jesus, and abundant grace was upon them all. For there was not a needy person among them, for all who were owners of land or houses would sell them and bring the proceeds of the sales and lay them at the apostles' feet, and they would be distributed to each as any had need."

During the onset of this tremendous need, the early church did a fantastic job of meeting the physical needs of their brothers and sisters in Christ. However, with the local Christians each selling their lands, homes, and possessions just to sustain the Hellenist Jews who remained in Jerusalem rather than going back to their own cities, it wouldn't be long before those temporary resources dried up.

JUST LEAVE ALREADY!

In Acts 5:1-10, Ananias and Sapphira forfeited their lives as the consequence for lying to the Holy Spirit. The result of this miracle was that great fear came over the whole church and over all who heard about it. Despite the Jerusalem church's partial obedience to God's revealed will of Great

Commission Discipleship, the Lord remained patient, blessing His people in countless ways.

It was at this time, however, that the effects of spiritual complacency began to truly take root there in Jerusalem.

In Acts 5:12-16, we see the fruit of God's blessing, but also the harbinger of problems in not being wholly obedient in venturing out into Judea and Samaria with the gospel. Take special notice of verse sixteen ("the cities in the vicinity of Jerusalem were coming together") in this passage of Scripture:

> "At the hands of the apostles many signs and wonders were taking place among the people; and they were all with one accord in Solomon's portico. But none of the rest dared to associate with them; however, the people held them in high esteem. And all the more believers in the Lord, multitudes of men and women, were constantly added to their number, to such an extent that they even carried the sick out into the streets and laid them on cots and pallets, so that when Peter came by at least his shadow might fall on any of them. Also the people from the *cities in the vicinity of Jerusalem* were coming together, bringing people who were sick or afflicted with unclean spirits, and they were all being healed" (emphasis mine).

Unfortunately, we learn from this passage that Jerusalem had become a Christian magnet of sorts. Outsiders needed to travel into Jerusalem rather than the good news branching out to them. Those living in the regions surrounding Jerusalem were forced to bring their sick, diseased, and demon-possessed loved ones into Jerusalem because no one was bothering to go to them. Obviously, that was a significant obstacle to the Great Commission, which is a mandate requiring world conquest, not merely local occupation.

Christ's plan for the church was to remain in Jerusalem only *until* they were clothed with the Holy Spirit. Unfortunately, the early believers chose to linger in Jerusalem rather than reaching out to all the nations.

Be sure you do not miss this critical truth. Divine Persecution of God's redeemed children will never make sense if you misunderstand the very reason it occurred.

The apostle Peter wrote:

> "But if anyone *suffers as a Christian*, he is not to be ashamed, *but is to glorify God* in this name. For it is time for *judgment to begin with the household of God*; and if it begins with us first, what will be the outcome for those who do not obey the gospel of God? And if it is with difficulty that the righteous is saved, what will be the outcome of the godless man and the sinner? Therefore, those also who *suffer according to the will of God* shall entrust their souls to a faithful Creator in doing what is right"[219] (emphasis mine).

WHAT GOD IS CONCERNED ABOUT MOST

Although it is often difficult to understand why, both physical and religious suffering is often according to the plan of God.

It's just the way God does it sometimes.

King Solomon wrote, "My Son, do not reject the

---

219 1 Peter 4:16–19

discipline of the LORD or loathe His reproof, for whom the LORD loves He reproves, even as a father corrects the son in whom he delights."[220]

It was this sort of correction which God had in mind when disciplining His children there in the city of Jerusalem.

Look, God certainly wasn't opposed to the gospel being proclaimed throughout the streets and synagogues of Jerusalem. The problem God had was that He wanted those things to be happening in Judea and Samaria as well. Though the Lord was granting miracles and healings and thousands of souls were being saved, God's revealed plan was for evangelistic ministry to be worldwide.

Remember, God is interested in the praise and worship of those who call upon His name. He isn't so concerned about whether or not Christianity is the world's most popular religion. God is not concerned about the popularity of your local church, nor is He remotely interested in how many names are listed in the church directory of a particular congregation. What God is most concerned about are the people whose names are written down in the Lamb's Book of Life!

Never forget that.

EVEN THE ENEMY KNEW IT WAS TIME FOR THE CHURCH TO MOVE ON

As if all this wasn't reason enough to leave Jerusalem, even the high priest complained about how saturated the city had become with the message of repentant faith in Jesus Christ alone. Upon arresting and forcing the apostles to appear

---

220 Proverbs 3:11-12

before the Council, the high priest confessed, "We gave you strict orders not to continue teaching in this name, and yet, you have *filled Jerusalem* with your teaching"[221] (emphasis mine).

You know you've done a thorough job of evangelizing a city when your worst critics openly confess that you have filled the entire city with the gospel. Jerusalem had become wonderfully saturated with the good news. It was now time for the church to move on to the next city.

Sadly, they refused to do just that.

WHERE THERE IS SMOKE, THERE IS FIRE

In Acts 6:1, it says: "Now at this time while the disciples were increasing in number, a complaint arose on the part of the Hellenistic Jews." The church in Jerusalem was increasing numerically to such an extent that elderly Hellenist widows were being overlooked in the daily serving of food.

This problem suggests that things were getting more than just slightly out of control there in the city. Christian cliques were beginning to form among God's children, and that is never a good thing.

Overcrowding and the shortage of daily resources became such a formidable problem that selfishness crept into the fellowship. There simply wasn't enough bread to go around. It became such an issue that the organized church was forced to select, dedicate, and appoint seven godly men to deal with the problem. One of those chosen was a man named Stephen, who was a man both full of faith and of the Holy Spirit.

---

221 Acts 5:28

Despite the fact that the disciples weren't being wholly obedient to our Lord's revealed will to take the gospel beyond Jerusalem, it is noteworthy that the Lord still honored the obedience that was present. God is so faithful to bless those who bless Him. No amount of faithfulness will ever go unnoticed or unblessed by our omniscient Rewarder.

In Acts 6:7, we then read, "The word of God kept on spreading; and the number of disciples continued to increase greatly *in Jerusalem*, and a great many of the priests were becoming obedient to the faith" (emphasis mine). Yet even here, in the midst of many conversions among the ranks of the Jewish priests, we see the problem at hand. Everything was happening *in Jerusalem*. No one was taking the gospel into Judea and Samaria.

Life was too comfortable. Jerusalem had become the soft pew of early church Christianity.

FAITHFUL REGARDLESS OF THE COST

In order to publicly glorify the Lord, sometimes you just have to accept the consequences and exit the place of refuge. Such was the case concerning the inspiring bravery of a young girl during China's Boxer Rebellion of 1900. It reminds me of how important remaining faithful to the Lord really is, even in the face of certain death.

During that rebellion, nearly one hundred students barricaded themselves inside a mission station. Every gate was blocked, except for one. The insurgents placed a wooden cross on the ground in front of that lone open gate. The students were told that if any of them came out and trampled the cross beneath their feet, they would be granted—not only their lives—but their freedom as well. Any who refused to do so, however, would be immediately shot and killed.

Each person was given the chance to decide for themselves.

Slowly, a handful of terrified students walked through the gate and trampled the cross beneath their feet. True to their word, the insurgents allowed those students to walk away unharmed.

Another girl soon followed, but instead of trampling the cross, she knelt before it in prayer, petitioning her Lord for strength in the midst of certain death. Having renewed her trust in the Savior, she stood up, made her way carefully around the cross, and walked toward the firing squad where she met her end. Emboldened by her example of faith in the Savior, each of the remaining students made their way out through the gate, around the cross, and into the hands of the firing squad where every one of them forfeited their lives for the glory of God.

I was reminded that it sometimes hurts being a worshipper of the true God. Being faithful to Christ may cost you your life in the end, but every one of us must pass through the gate and decide whom we will serve: Jehovah, or the god of self-preservation.

PLAYING TRUTH OR DARE WITH GOD

Jesus' revealed will for the early church was that they would be His "witnesses both in Jerusalem, and in all Judea and Samaria, and even to the remotest part of the earth."[222]

---

222 Acts 1:8

The mandate of intentional discipleship was crystal-clear. It was not a suggestion or even a sanctified recommendation. The issue was simply whether they'd be obedient or disobedient to the commands of their Lord.

Sadly, the Jerusalem church in Acts chapters two through seven chose convenience rather than unyielding allegiance. And so—in His sovereignty—God called their bluff.

After debating in a synagogue filled with unbelieving Jews, Stephen was dragged away, brought before the Council, and required to give a defense of the charges put against him. Some lying Jews then induced other Jewish liars to accuse Stephen of blasphemy and of speaking against both the Law and the customs that Moses handed down. Upon gazing at the man who had a face like that of an angel, the high priest asked Stephen if the charges were true.

Rather than respond with a simple "No," Stephen chose to preach a sermon. He ended his plea by flipping the accusations onto the Council and actually indicted them with the sin of blasphemy, of breaking God's Law and of murdering the Righteous One. Apparently the Council didn't appreciate Stephen's opinion, because they began gnashing their teeth at him. Crying out with a loud voice, they covered their ears and rushed at him with one impulse. As they drove him out of the city, they fulfilled Stephen's accusation of them.

Indeed, they were just like their fathers.

This heated event sparked the inferno of religious persecution against the early church there in the city of Jerusalem. And make no mistake about it. God was behind it all.

FRONT ROW SEATS TO MURDER

No matter how many times I read the final verses of Acts chapter seven, I never cease to be both shocked and perplexed at how God peeled away the heavens just to get a front row seat to watch His servant get murdered. For me, above all other passages in holy Scripture, this one stands as the trademark text proving that God was not only fully aware of the persecution of His people, but that He was also in complete control over it.

As the Council gnashed their teeth and rushed the soon-to-be-martyr out of the city, Scripture says of Stephen, "Being full of the Holy Spirit, he gazed intently into heaven and saw the glory of God, and Jesus standing at the right hand of God; and he said, 'Behold, I see the heavens opened up and the Son of Man standing at the right hand of God.'"[223] As the religious sinners hurled their deadly stones, Stephen called on the Lord, saying, "Lord Jesus, receive my spirit!"[224]

Picture in your mind's eye all that was taking place at that moment. Stephen was being throttled, pressed down, and thrown to the ground. Dozens of angry men were standing over him, gnashing their teeth, spitting with furious rage, and snatching fist-sized rocks from the dirt. One by one, they began launching their missiles at a defenseless man.

During the final moments of his agony, Stephen gazed into the sky and saw "the glory of God, and Jesus" staring down at him from Heaven.[225] As each stone cut, lacer-

---

223 Acts 7:55-56
224 Acts 7:59
225 Acts 7:55

ated, and smashed into the bones of his face, head, neck, shoulders, back, and chest, the bloodied Stephen encouraged his murderers to look up into the sky, because right over their heads was none other than "the Son of Man standing at the right hand of God."[226]

Stephen didn't beg God's rescue, and God offered no assistance. Stephen didn't plead for divine clemency, and God didn't grant him any, either. Stephen didn't demand vengeance upon his enemies, and God tendered none. God the Father and God the Son were watching the proceedings, making sure everything happened precisely the way it was supposed to. Every detail was accounted for. Nothing outside of God's sovereignty was occurring at that moment. The omnipotent Lord of Lords is seen here in this passage mercifully ensuring that the religious persecution didn't go even an inch beyond what it was supposed to.

Question: Do you have a problem with this?

GOD IS NEVER UNJUST

Let's be clear. God never caused the Council to sin, nor did He influence them to murder. God did, however, remove His hand of restraint for a time. This removal of restraint is what allowed the Council to be as utterly sinful as their wicked minds wanted to be. And their depraved minds certainly lusted for the sin of murder.

It was all happening according to plan. God permitted every detail. It was God's will for Stephen's life that fateful day.

---

226 Acts 7:56

I know many Christians today probably have a major problem with this. But please notice that Stephen didn't. He knew God is sovereign. Never once did he even consider shaking his fist toward the sky as he stared into the eyes of his beloved Savior. Neither should we. We need to be passionate disciples, not irreverent critics.

As you know, there are many things in the Bible that are difficult to understand. Some are just plain hard to swallow. As the apostle Peter wrote in 2 Peter 3:16, there are "some things hard to understand, which the untaught and unstable distort, as they do also the rest of the Scriptures." Yet it would be downright improper—no, outright sinful—to hide the truth about God's holy character or attempt to describe Him in a way that is out of harmony with what the Word clearly teaches.

God is immensely merciful and more compassionate than we could ever begin to comprehend. But it is rather false prophet-like to consciously distort the holy character of God just so we can cling to the false idol of what we want God to be like. You might not like it. You might not understand it. But do yourself a favor and let God be God. There isn't enough room on Heaven's throne for the both of you.

HOW TO NOT BLAME GOD

It was for a similar reason that God said to Eliphaz the Temanite, "My wrath is kindled against you and against your two friends, because you have *not spoken of Me what is right* as My servant Job has"[227] (emphasis mine).

---

227 Job 42:7

After God commanded Job's three foolish counselors to offer sacrifices and have Job pray for them, God then announced, "For I will accept him so that I may not do to you according to your folly, because you have *not spoken of Me what is right*, as My servant Job has"[228] (emphasis mine).

If there was anyone on the face of the planet who ever had reason to blame God for his circumstances, it was Job. Even God Himself confessed to Satan that, regarding Job, "There is no one like him on the earth, a blameless and upright man, fearing God and turning away from evil."[229] Even so, what did God permit the devil to do in order to manifest the quality of Job's holy character? He allowed Satan to cause some ungodly foreigners to attack and plunder his oxen and donkeys, for lightning to fall from the sky and burn up his sheep and servants, for the Chaldeans to steal his camels and slay his servants, and for a great wind to rise up and kill every one of his sons and daughters.

Yes, if anyone had a reason to question the integrity of God's actions, it was Job.

But how did godly Job respond to the God-ordained atrocities that befell him?

In Job 1:20 it says:

> "Then Job arose and tore his robe and shaved his head, and fell to the ground and *worshipped*. He said, 'Naked I came from my mother's womb and naked I shall return there. The LORD gave and the LORD has taken away. *Blessed be the name of the LORD.*'"

228 Job 42:8
229 Job 1:8

> Through all this *Job did not sin nor did he blame God.*
> (emphasis mine)

Job didn't raise his fist toward the clouds and curse God. Rather, he did what we all should be doing today—blessed God's holy name in passionate worship.

Yet even that wasn't the extent of Job's suffering. God had a lot more misery in store for him to endure.

INFLICTED BY GOD

In the very next chapter, God and Satan had another conversation about Job.

Satan said to God, "Put forth *Your hand* now, and touch his bone and his flesh; he will curse You to Your face" (emphasis mine).[230] After God permitted Job's body to be brutally injured "with sore boils from the sole of his foot to the crown of his head," Job still maintained his integrity.[231]

While he was scraping his marred skin with a broken potsherd, Job's wife told him to "'Curse God and die!' Yet he said to her, 'You speak as one of the foolish women speaks. Shall we indeed accept good from God and *not accept adversity?*' In all this *Job did not sin with his lips*" (emphasis mine).[232]

Yes, there was good reason for God to proclaim about Job, "There is no one like him on earth, a blameless and upright man fearing God and turning away from evil."[233]

Beloved, it is only proper and good to be found speaking

---

230 Job 2:5
231 Job 2:7
232 Job 2:9-10
233 Job 2:3

and teaching what is right concerning God and His holy character. We would do well to remember that God said, "'For My thoughts are not your thoughts, nor are your ways My ways,' declares the LORD. 'For as the heavens are higher than the earth, so are My ways higher than your ways and My thoughts than your thoughts.'"[234]

ONWARD TO GREENER PASTURES

At this crucial point in the life of the early church, God began to execute (pun intended) phase two of His revealed plan for Great Commission Discipleship. In a strikingly similar way to how the Council drove Stephen out of the city, the Lord—Himself—rushed His people out of the city so that the mission of evangelizing the lost would move on to phase two (Judea and Samaria).

As far as Scripture tells us, Stephen became the very first believer to ever actually leave the city of Jerusalem. For the two-year period between the ascension of Jesus Christ and Stephen's murder in Acts chapter seven, Scripture doesn't even suggest that any of the Christians ever left the city to go back to their own homes, left to evangelize the areas surrounding Jerusalem, or even went on an afternoon stroll outside the city gates.

God had certainly been patient with the church there in Jerusalem.

Notice what it says immediately after Stephen's death in Acts 8:1, "And on that day a great persecution began against *the church in Jerusalem*, and they were scattered

---

234 Isaiah 55:8-9

throughout the regions of *Judea and Samaria,* except the apostles" (emphasis mine).

Where did Jesus command His disciples to take the gospel after Jerusalem? Judea and Samaria. Where did the Lord scatter His people with this persecution in Acts chapter eight? Judea and Samaria. God is holy! He is serious about this Great Commission business. With the introduction of religious persecution, the Lord scattered His people so that they'd move toward being wholly obedient to His revealed will for their lives.

There is so much to learn from all these events. I pray that the contemporary American church learns it soon, before the Lord decides to call our bluff. Don't you?

CHAPTER ELEVEN

THE LOCAL CHURCH: IGNORANT, RACIST, AND REDEEMED

"In everything give thanks; for this is God's will for you in Christ Jesus." (1 Thessalonians 5:18)

"Lesson one: God wants all people—no matter their names or numbers. Lesson two: God does incredible things to demonstrate that first point." —Ronnie Floyd

AN INMATE APPROACHED me after a prison chapel service one evening and asked me to pray with him. After conversing about what I had preached on that evening, he said something that—although other inmates have said similar things in the past—still struck me as profound. And true.

He said, "You know, I'm convinced that God had to take everything away from me before I'd ever listen to Him. I mean, I never would've read the Bible or gone to church if I hadn't been put in jail."

How would you respond if someone said that to you?

I often find myself just nodding in agreement.

Undoubtedly that young man forfeited everything he called his own, including many of the people he cared about most. After numerous weeks of being locked in a crowded cellblock—mulling over the results of poor decisions—that young man concluded that God had orchestrated all of the events in order to bring him to the point where he was convinced it was the only way he would ever think about God. He didn't blame God one bit for his new mailing address, for he knew he was in jail because of his own sin. Yet he also wouldn't be dissuaded that God's hand was in all of it.

And I certainly wasn't going to try to convince him otherwise.

Two Widows Enter a Village

In the book of Ruth, Naomi also came to a point when she, likewise, had to admit God was intimately involved in the tragedies of life.

After her husband, Elimelech, moved their family into the land of Moab during a time of severe famine, untold events eventually led to the death of her husband and two sons. As Naomi arrived back in her hometown of Bethlehem, the local women came together and were astounded by the outer shell of their old friend. Responding to their disbelief, she replied,

> "Do not call me Naomi; call me Mara, for *the Almighty has dealt very bitterly with me*. I went out full, but *the LORD has brought me back empty*. Why

> do you call me Naomi, since *the LORD has wit-*
> *nessed against me and the Almighty has afflicted me?"*
> (emphasis mine)[235]

Although the circumstances for the early church in the book of Acts were quite different than that of Elimelech and Naomi, no doubt those early believers became fully aware that it was the Almighty who had afflicted them. Yet even in the midst of divine persecution, the Lord was never really against His beloved children. In fact, He was very much preparing to bless them immensely.

THE BLESSINGS OF FURTHER OBEDIENCE

In Acts 8:4-5 we learn that "those who had been scattered went about preaching the word. Philip went down to Samaria and began proclaiming Christ to them." Where was the church supposed to take the gospel after Jerusalem? Judea and Samaria. Where did Philip go to proclaim Christ? Samaria.

With the divine prodding stick of religious persecution came the fruit of holy compliance.

Outside the comfortable confines of Jerusalem, the rest of the unsaved world was finally having the good news preached to it, as the Lord scattered His people. Philip preached the gospel to Samaria, and the crowds were responding positively to what he said. The Samaritans received Philip's message with open gladness, to the point that "there was much rejoicing in that city."[236]

Word traveled back to Jerusalem that Samaria had

---

235 Ruth 1:20,21
236 Acts 8:8

received the Word of God. The apostles heard this and sent Peter and John to them in order that they might also receive the gift of the Holy Spirit. Yet for some reason, once the Samaritan believers had received the Holy Spirit's gift, the apostles walked back to Jerusalem. In their ignorance they still didn't comprehend the fullness of the Great Commission in that they needed to continue on, even to the remotest part of the Earth.

Don't Go Back Home Just Yet

Perhaps the reason the apostles didn't each choose a Judean city and make it their own evangelistic headquarters was so that no one would say anything like, "I am of Paul," or "I am of Apollos."[237] Or perhaps they simply believed their primary ministry was now to be limited only to native Jews living inside Jerusalem, seeing that most of the Hellenist Christians had been scattered abroad via persecution.

Nevertheless, we need to understand that what ultimately hindered them from being wholly obedient in going to the remotest part of the earth was *ignorance*.

Ignorance of God's plan to save the loathsome Gentiles, that is.

Jerusalem was not difficult for the apostles to comprehend. There were plenty of native Jews living there. With the stinging rod of divine persecution, they quickly understood that half-breed Jews scattered throughout Judea and Samaria were a part of God's Great Commission plan as well. But that's pretty much where their comprehension of Great Commission Discipleship ended.

---

237 1 Corinthians 3:4

The early church was initially excited about ministry, but only to the point that it was convenient. When God called their bluff, they knew they needed to venture into Judea and Samaria with the gospel. So off they went. But from that point forward, spiritual complacency was no longer the issue at hand. Ignorance now reigned supreme.

Oh, and racism reigned as well. Yes, the sinful racism which existed among God's people.

Regrettably, the Jews didn't understand that when Jesus said they would be His witnesses even to the remotest part of the Earth, He meant they were to take the gospel to the Gentiles. And yet, God was patiently leading them to the place of comprehension. The Lord was preparing to lift the veil of their evangelistic ignorance once and for all.

JUST STAY OUT OF JERUSALEM ALREADY

Shortly after the initial scattering of the church into Judea and Samaria, an angel of the Lord spoke to Philip in Acts 8:26, telling him to "Get up" and travel to a road "that descends from Jerusalem to Gaza." Philip got up and went, and met an Egyptian eunuch who had "come to Jerusalem to worship."[238] Notice that the Egyptian eunuch traveled all the way to the city of Jerusalem specifically to worship the God of Israel. The eunuch was there for religious worship, not business or entertainment.

It is fascinating that the Lord didn't send any of the twelve apostles to this eunuch while he was in Jerusalem. The Lord was prepared to wait patiently until the eunuch

---

238 Acts 8:27

was outside the city and on his way back to Egypt before sending anyone to make him into a disciple of Jesus Christ.

There was no way God was going to let anyone share the good news with that eunuch until he was outside Jerusalem and on his way back home. Through this incident, God was teaching His people that they needed to get up and *go* and not wait for the professionals (i.e. the apostles) to do the work.

After he had evangelized and baptized the eunuch, Philip was supernaturally transported by the Lord to other out-lying areas, beginning at "Azotus, and as he passed through he kept preaching the gospel to all the cities until he came to Caesarea."[239]

WHAT WOULD YOU HAVE DONE?

If I were Philip, the first thing I'd have done after leaving the eunuch's presence would have been to go into Jerusalem, find the twelve apostles, and tell them all about the miracle God just did. He wasn't that far from the gates of Jerusalem, after all—just a quick jog up the road. But that wasn't God's will. Not even close.

The Lord wanted ministry happening outside Jerusalem, not inside only. It was time for the Jews to understand that the spread of the gospel would take place all around the world and not to the residents of Jerusalem solely.

I see a lot of application from this text for the American Church today. God certainly wants His people inside local churches, fellowshipping with one another and studying the Word. But He doesn't want that to be the gist of our

---

239 Acts 8:40

Great Commission labor. We also need to be actively involved in evangelistic ministry, rather than leaving that grand work up to the professionals (i.e. the pastors).

Like Philip, we need to be obedient to the Lord and fulfill His revealed will for our lives.

THE RIGHT TOOL FOR THE JOB

In Acts chapter nine, we learn about the conversion of Saul, who was the perpetrator in hearty agreement with Stephen's murder back in Acts 8:1.

Saul of Tarsus (who later changed his name to Paul) was on his way to Damascus looking for any man or woman who claimed to be Christian. Damascus was the capital of Syria, located about 160 miles northeast of Jerusalem. Apparently a significant number of Hellenist Jews fled there after the persecution in Jerusalem. The news of the Christian message had traveled quite a distance from its original starting point in Jerusalem. But the Lord wasn't satisfied yet.

Jesus revealed Himself to Saul of Tarsus, telling him that he'd be told what he must do. Christ then spoke to a disciple named Ananias and commanded him to lay hands on Saul, saying, "Go, for he is a chosen instrument of Mine, to bear My name before the *Gentiles and kings* and the sons of Israel"[240] (emphasis mine).

We see here that the Lord was beginning to mold His chosen vessel in order to scatter the gospel message beyond even Judea and Samaria, so that it would reach the remotest part of the earth.

Question: What do you think about that?

---

240 Acts 9:15

Isn't it ironic that the Lord chose to use one of the original instruments of persecution (Saul of Tarsus) to scatter the life-changing message to a Gentile people he would have no doubt deemed unworthy of even coming into contact with? The instrument of Stephen's persecution became the hammer used by God to spread the gospel to a people Saul would have totally despised.

Such is the mind of our Lord.

GOD'S WILL MEANS NO
REST FOR THE WEARY

As the church began venturing into the outlying areas of Judea and Samaria—preaching the gospel in every city they entered—they were transitioning away from *partial* obedience and moving toward *total* obedience. With this change in both attitude and action, the Lord yanked back the reins of divine persecution and granted them peace for a season.

Notice what the Scripture says in Acts 9:31: "So the church throughout all *Judea* and Galilee and *Samaria* enjoyed peace, being built up; and going on in the fear of the Lord and in the comfort of the Holy Spirit, it continued to increase" (emphasis mine). Once the gospel was being sent into phase two of the Lord's revealed will for Great Commission Discipleship, the church enjoyed both peace and numerical growth. They were beginning to understand—literally—what it means to go on in the fear of the Lord.

Although the scattered believers were beginning to more fully comprehend what the Lord required of them, they failed to grasp the extent of Great Commission Discipleship in its totality. Sadly, they believed the gospel was reserved primarily for the Jews. They apparently interpreted the concept of "all the nations" and the "remotest part of the Earth" to mean only Jews living in those places. They couldn't see past their racial and ethnic bigotries. They were just too racist to see the plain truth before them.

And so the Lord needed to teach them an important lesson. That lesson began on a rooftop in Joppa with a student named Peter.

As for Me and My House, We Will Serve the Lord

It's strange to think that the Jewish Christians didn't understand their missionary outreach was to include the Gentiles. It was a veiled mystery, after all.

Since God is the Creator of all things and all people, wouldn't He also be the only true God of the Gentiles as well? Of course He is. Unfortunately, most of the Jews (including the apostles) believed the salvation of Gentile nations to be outside the realm of Christ's Great Commission plan. They simply did not believe this was God's will for the gospel.

In order to convince His people otherwise, the Lord needed to reveal this to them in a miraculous way.

He did just that.

A Gentile named Cornelius, who was a Roman centurion and, therefore, normally hated by the Jews, was also "a devout man and one who feared God with all his household, and gave many alms to the Jewish people and prayed to God continually."[241] Cornelius was no ordinary sinner,

---

241 Acts 10:2

let alone an ordinary Gentile. He feared God, worshipping the Lord despite the racial and ethnic boundaries erected around him by the people of God's chosen nation. Even though he wasn't a Jew, Cornelius' prayers and alms had ascended as a memorial before God.

It was this non-Jewish, Roman centurion—and his entire household as well—whom God used to teach Peter that He is the God of the Gentiles, also.

More Than a New Diet

Peter received a vision from the Lord when he fell into a trance on that rooftop in Joppa. The vision he received contained both clean and unclean animals.

God's message to Peter was clear: "Get up, Peter, kill and eat!" [242] Peter responded by saying, "By no means, Lord, for I have never eaten anything unholy and unclean."[243] The voice of the Lord then came to him three times, saying, "What God has cleansed, no longer consider unholy."[244]

In other words, Peter and the other circumcised Jewish believers had considered the pagan Gentiles to be entirely unclean, unholy, and, therefore, altogether disqualified from being recipients of the gospel. Yet, God was teaching the apostle that He has the power, the authority, and the desire to make the Gentiles *holy* and *clean*.

So, Peter and six Jewish witnesses traveled all the way to Caesarea to see what the Lord had in mind.

Being accompanied by the men sent from Cornelius, they informed Peter that Cornelius was "divinely directed

---

242 Acts 10:13
243 Acts 10:14
244 Acts 10:15

by a holy angel to send for you to come to his house and hear a message from you."[245] It is important to note that, although Cornelius and those of his household were spiritually zealous for the things of the Lord, they were, nevertheless, unsaved.[246]

God willed for Peter to travel into foreign enemy territory, rather than Cornelius and his household traveling to, for example, the city of Jerusalem. God was about to—once and for all—remove the veil of Peter's ignorance regarding Great Commission Discipleship. This event would prove to Peter the necessity for total obedience in that he needed to go into the entire world and preach the gospel to all creation.

A Serious Flaw in the Plan

In Acts 10:28 we learn from Peter's own mouth about the profound ignorance he and the other circumcised believers had with regards to God's redemptive plan. He said to them, "You yourselves know how *unlawful* it is for a man who is a Jew to *associate* with a foreigner or to *visit* him; and yet God has shown me that I should not call any man *unholy* or *unclean*" (emphasis mine).

Whoa! Hold on a minute. Did you catch what Peter just said?

He said that—according to the common Jewish belief—it was *unlawful* to even *associate* with or *visit* a foreigner! How in the world can you fulfill the Great Commission to every nation if you consider everyone else in the world to be unclean, unholy, and even unworthy to visit with?

245 Acts 10:22
246 Acts 11:14

Yes, the Jewish Christians had much to learn about to what it means to truly love your neighbor as yourself.

French reformer John Calvin once commented on this issue of Christian racism when he wrote, "How necessary it was that the apostles should be distinctly informed of the calling of the Gentiles, is evident from this consideration, that even after having received the command, they felt the greatest horror at approaching them, as if by doing so they polluted themselves and their doctrine."[247]

How very true.

Upon hearing Cornelius speak, Peter began to more fully comprehend the Lord's revealed plan for Great Commission Discipleship, regarding how the Gentiles are also a part of that mission. Peter linked the obvious correlation of the "unclean" and "unholy" animals from his rooftop vision with the so-called unclean and unholy Gentiles.

Peter then declared, "I most certainly *understand now* that God is not one to show partiality, but in *every nation* the man who fears Him and does what is right is welcome to Him"[248] (emphasis mine). Notice the nationality of the people Peter now says are welcome to God: *Every nation.*

He's starting to get it. It's beginning to click.

He even articulates this newfound mystery further in verse forty-three, saying, "All the prophets bear witness that through His name *everyone* who believes in Him receives forgiveness of sins" (emphasis mine).

---

247 John Calvin, Calvin's Commentaries, A Harmony of the Synoptic Gospels (Calvin Publications, Inc.), page 588.
248 Acts 10:34

GOD SHOWS NO PARTIALITY

Isn't it fantastic that the biblical gospel promises forgiveness of sins to everyone who believes in Him, regardless of their ethnicity, nationality, or even the color of their skin? It doesn't matter if a person is black, white, Asian, Hispanic, rich or poor, smart or dumb, famous or common. The gospel is readily available to all presidents, dictators, queens, white- and blue-collared workers, and even homeless drunks passed out in a dirty gutter. Despite one's ethnicity or circumstance, if a person turns from their sin and trusts in Jesus Christ alone, God will shower them with His matchless grace.

What an awesome message to proclaim!

The gospel of Jesus Christ, which began in Jerusalem—then transitioned into Judea and Samaria as the Lord unleashed divine persecution—eventually worked its way to non-Jewish people as well. This all occurred once Peter began to preach to all the nations, beginning with a despised Roman centurion.

But as wonderful as all this was, the Lord wasn't finished with His divine lesson just yet. There was still a bit of convincing yet to be done back in good old Jerusalem.

AN APPLE FOR THE TEACHER

During Peter's message to Cornelius and his household, the Lord worked in a miraculous way. He did so in order to demonstrate that the faith and adoption of the Gentile believers was no different in either quality or substance when compared to that of the Jewish believers during Pentecost in Acts chapter two.

Acts 10:44-45 says, "While Peter was still speaking these words, the Holy Spirit fell upon all those who were listening to the message. All the circumcised believers who came with Peter were amazed, because the gift of the Holy Sprit had been poured out on the Gentiles also." Peter and the other six circumcised believers witnessed the entire household "speaking in tongues and exalting God," and Peter announced, "Surely no one can refuse the water for these to be baptized who have received the Holy Spirit just as we did, can he?"[249]

After all was said and done that day in Caesarea, the Lord had accomplished many, many things. He had educated Peter (the apostle upon whom He said He would build His Church), and He yanked away the ethnic curtain, revealing the mystery that the Gentiles are also a piece of that Great Commission puzzle.

He visibly demonstrated this to the other six circumcised believers as well so that the fact would be confirmed by the testimony of at least two or three witnesses.

Furthermore, He showed us through the written Word that God desires all people to know Him and to come before Him in the fear of the Lord.

If you are a genuine Christian, then you serve a most awesome and compassionate God!

THE MYSTERY REVEALED

All that remained now was for Peter to convince the other racist apostles and circumcised believers back in Jerusalem

---

249 Acts 10:46-47

to embrace the reviled Gentiles as their fellow brothers and sisters. No problem, right?

Acts 11:1 says, "The apostles and the brethren who were throughout Judea heard that the Gentiles also had received the word of God." The only problem, however, was that when Peter arrived back in Jerusalem, "those who were circumcised took issue with him."[250]

It is baffling to me when Christians respond with a cold indifference—rather than pure joy—when they hear about people in other places around the world getting saved. Racial hatred can often run deep, even among believers. Yet this should never be the case.

This was a crucial moment for both the early church and the entire Great Commission as a whole. Would the other apostles and Jewish Christians go against the grain of everything they had once assumed to be true? Would the Jewish believers embrace the despised Gentiles into their fellowship, no longer considering them unholy, unclean, or excluded from God's redemptive plan? Would the Jews agree to cast off their racial bigotries and be wholly obedient to the revealed Great Commission? Would they begin to finally love their Gentile neighbors as themselves?

Let's find out.

Peter explained to the other apostles and circumcised believers about all that had taken place, beginning with the vision in Joppa and ending with the Gentiles receiving the Holy Spirit, just as He had fallen upon them during Pentecost. What happened next serves as the first public

---

250 Acts 11:2

declaration and subsequent acceptance of the Gentiles into the fellowship as co-heirs of the grace of God.

Peter declared:

> "Therefore if God gave to them the same gift as He gave to us also after believing in the Lord Jesus Christ, who was I that I could stand in God's way?" When they heard this, they quieted down and glorified God, saying, "Well, then, God has granted to the Gentiles also the repentance that leads to life."[251]

And there you have it. No one anticipated or ever expected it to happen, but neither would anyone argue with God, deny that the miracle had occurred, or say anything against the testimony of Peter and the other six witnesses.

God's revealed will for Great Commission Discipleship was that it would first begin in Jerusalem when the disciples received power from on high, and it did.

The gospel was then to travel into the regions of Judea and Samaria, and it did—though the Lord had to scatter His people with divine persecution in order to make it happen.

Finally, after lifting the veil and washing away the scales of ignorance, God revealed to the Jewish believers that He loves the Gentiles just as much as them. They are also an integral part of His compassionate grace.

What a merciful God we serve.

---

251 Acts 11:17–18

THE FRUIT OF A WELL-TENDED HARVEST

Lastly, we learn from Acts 11:19 and following that each of these spiritual blessings stemmed from "those who were scattered because of the persecution that occurred in connection with Stephen."[252] Luke, penning the wonderful book of Acts under the inspiration of the Holy Spirit, tied all these events back to the original persecution that commenced with Stephen's death.

It doesn't get any more obvious than that, folks. God was sovereign through—and over—all those events, especially the trials and tribulations His adopted children were forced to endure.

There were some believing Jewish disciples who felt called to speak "the word to no one except to Jews alone," but there were also some men who traveled to various cities "and began speaking to the Greeks also, preaching the Lord Jesus."[253] Yet each person was called to fulfill his or her own Great Commission ministry to one people group or another.

So are you today as well. This is most definitely God's revealed will for your life today.

The fruit of such widespread obedience in making disciples of all the nations is crystal clear, because the Scripture then says, "The hand of the Lord was with them, and a large number who believed turned to the Lord."[254]

Question: What was the conclusion to all this evangelism and obedience to Great Commission Discipleship? How

---

252 Act 11:19
253 Acts 11:19–20
254 Acts 11:21

did the Lord react to the church's obedience of leaving Jerusalem and venturing out into Judea and Samaria and finally to the remotest part of the earth?

Answer: The Lord was with them, and a large number of sinners turned to the Lord.

This was the ultimate and lofty goal of our Savior. This is the reason we're still inhaling and exhaling right now. The means in which He chose to bring it to pass were through earthen pots of clay like you and me. He chose to spread the gospel verbally through people willing to be wholly obedient, going forth in the fear of the Lord, traveling to the remotest part of the Earth.

So the question remains: What does this all have to do with you? What bearing does it have on contemporary American Christian today? Why should any of us care, in other words?

GOD'S WILL IS THAT YOU NOT TEST HIM

As a non-Jew, the gospel came to me because someone cared enough to share it with me. The good news is offered and available to you because the Lord directed his apostles some 2,000 years ago that you (most likely a Gentile) are an integral part of His redemptive plan.

I was told the good news of our Lord and—by His grace alone—responded with repentant faith. This all happened because a handful of believers were faithful to step out of their comfort zone and share the message of all messages with me. They chose to get off their comfy pews and be intentionally deliberate about the beautiful mission of disciple-making.

Imagine the harvest of spiritual fruit to be gathered if more believers—such as yourself and those in your own local church—would do the same to walk by faith and not by sight. Imagine what wonderful things the Lord would do through us if we cast off the dingy cloak of spiritual complacency and chose to worship God with uncompromising obedience.

Just imagine.

Allow me to throw out a question or two, and believe me, I keep asking these same questions of myself over and over again.

- How has your relationship with the Lord been lately?

- How are you progressing in your personal discipleship time?

- How is your prayer life? (Do you even have a prayer life at the moment?)

- Are you being continually conformed to the image of Christ, or are you coasting along on spiritual cruise control?

- Do you think your churchgoing lifestyle is closer to that of a tare or wheat?

- Are you involved in any ministry that serves the Church and edifies the saints? (Why or why not?)

- Are you helping other believers around you to grow in their faith in order to become more obedient disciples themselves?

- Are you content to sit back on comfortable pews in stained-glass church buildings, rather than share the gospel with unbelievers in order to make disciples of our Lord Jesus Christ?

- Are you or the other churchgoers you know hanging out in holy huddles, or are you passionately making disciples and warning sinners to flee from the wrath to come?

- If you're not evangelizing the lost or building up the faith of the redeemed, then what exactly *are* you doing?

We should each confess and repent of all our sinful omissions. "Therefore, to one who knows the right thing to do and *does not do it*, to him it is sin"[255] (emphasis mine).

We should all be ashamed of ourselves for not telling more people about the judgment to come, and for keeping the glorious good news of salvation practically a secret from those around us. That is not why Jesus died on the cross, rose from the grave, and empowered us with supernatural spiritual gifts.

We need to reexamine our priorities, both individually and collectively in our own local church assemblies. Church was designed by God to be a place for worship,

---

255 James 4:17

fellowship, discipleship, and evangelism. It's not a country club for entertainment purposes, and it's certainly not a place to check *God* off our spiritual to-do list.

THE GOD OF SECOND CHANCES

Fellow Christian, no doubt you're aware that the commands of Great Commission Discipleship apply to you. They apply to each of us. God's merciful grace is the greatest news anyone could ever hear.

So why aren't we shouting it from the rooftops?

Jesus took upon Himself God's wrath for our sins. All He wants us to do is tell others about it, leaving the results of our ministries to Him. We have no excuse for the sin of partial obedience, which is a sin of wickedness, divination, and idolatry. We each know the truth and our consciences are bearing witness against us.

I believe many of God's children (this author included, I'm afraid) will have much to give account for when we stand before the risen Savior at the Judgment Seat of Christ. There are nearly seven billion people living on this floating ball of dirt. It's not as though we need to travel very far to find a sinner or two. In many cases, it might be best to start with the person staring back at you in the mirror.

Praise the Lord that He remains the ever-living God of second chances!

CHAPTER TWELVE

THE WILL OF GOD
IN MOTION

*"A woman named Lydia, from the city of Thyatira,
a seller of purple fabrics, a worshiper of God, was listening; and the Lord opened her heart to respond
to the things spoken by Paul." (Acts 16:14)*

*"Jesus was not content to simply say what was true. Being
right was not enough. Being biblical was not enough. Being
exegetically correct was not enough. This was not his purpose in coming. He came to seek and to save that which
was lost. And he communicated to that end. Jesus understood what too many of us have either forgotten or were never
told in the first place. To seek and to save the lost, you must
first capture their attention. That's exactly what he did. As
his body, that's what we must do as well." —Andy Stanley*

I WAS JUST AN ordinary fifteen-year-old blasphemer the
first time anyone cared enough to share the gospel
with me. It was the first time anyone ever showed me real
Christian love.

I don't remember most of the details from that blessed encounter, but I do recall one thing as clear as day. When the two Christians ended the conversation and turned to walk away, I was more jealous at that moment than I've ever been in my life since.

By the time I turned fifteen years old, I was neck-deep in the mire of teenage rebellion.

It was just another weekend during the high school year, and I was hanging out on a street corner one night with three of my depraved friends. Like practically everyone else that evening, my friends and I were doing all we could to enjoy the passing pleasures of sin for a season. It was called *The Ave*, and cars packed with wild teenagers cruised up and down the boulevard, struttin' their stuff. Those without a driver's license (me, for example) were forced to hang out in groups along the sidewalk, waiting for mischief to cross our path.

It usually did.

We'd spent most of that night drinking alcohol and smoking marijuana. My buddies and I were acting totally obnoxious, when suddenly the crowd of people parted down the middle like a human Red Sea. Through the midst of fleeing sinners, two blond-haired teenagers marched toward us with a mission. Or more specifically— a Great Commission. They were part of a larger church group that walked along *The Ave* sharing their Christian faith with anyone who cared to listen.

Or at least anyone who wouldn't walk away.

It was obvious those two kids were out of place. The Bibles in their hands simply did not belong. They were like two beams of blinding light shining in a dark cave. Like everyone else in the immediate vicinity, I tried to scurry out of their way. Yet for some crazy reason, my feet just wouldn't move. How strange.

Those two teenagers walked over to us, and, even today, I can picture the nervous tension etched on their faces. Despite the fear of man, however, they began sharing with us about things like sin, Hell, Heaven, and faith in Jesus Christ.

I wish I could say that my friends and I were courteous to those two—even civil—but to do so would be to lie. Though we stopped short of spitting in their faces and smacking their Bibles to the pavement, we weren't what you would call *encouraging*, either.

My buddies and I blasphemed, joked, blasphemed, cursed, blasphemed, poked fun at, blasphemed, and otherwise challenged those two Christians with blasphemous questions like, "Oh yeah, so who made God then?" Every time the conversation veered toward the direction of my sinfulness, I dodged and parried with another stump-the-Christian question.

I'm ashamed even today.

I don't remember much else from that brief conversation, but the two budding evangelists eventually thanked us for talking with them and then shuffled over to the next huddle of teenage drunkards. However, I shall never forget the thought that pierced my conscience when they turned to walk away. I remember being handcuffed with envy, thinking, *I wish I could have what they have.*

My buddies and I discussed the conversation a few minutes

later. We each agreed that it took guts to go around talking to people about God like that. Though thoroughly unrepentant, we couldn't help but be impressed. Actually, I'm not sure who was more impressed with those two young and nervous Christians—me or my depraved friends.

Today, whenever I share the gospel with someone who blasphemes the things of God, I instantly recall the longing I felt that evening as a teenager. When the conversation is finished, I walk away knowing that the person I just witnessed to will still be thinking about their eternity for weeks to come. Maybe even years.

And then I smile.

WATERED WITH RADICAL LOVE

That first seed was sown into the soil of my heart, and— seven years later when I was a senior in college—the Lord decided it should bear fruit.

A student co-worker of mine in college lived two floors below me in our dormitory and was a faithful Christian armed with a godly lifestyle. She and I became friends because of our jobs (we were each Resident Assistants on our dormitory floors), and shortly after meeting for the first time, I learned she was a Christian.

For the second time now, I wish that I could say I was somewhat courteous to the few Christians who crossed my path. But I simply wasn't.

Over the weeks that followed, I debated with her about many spiritual things. Yet she firmly held her ground. In fact, whenever she didn't have an immediate answer to one of my stump-the-Christian questions, she would stay awake that night looking up the answers in her Bible. She'd then write me a letter containing all the answers—including the corresponding Bible verse references—and slide the letter under my door in the middle of the night. More often than not, those letters were five or six pages long. Written on both sides of the paper. Written by hand.

I didn't deserve such kindness.

Although I didn't always agree (or, rather, *want* to agree) with her answers, I couldn't help but be impressed by how kind she was to do that for me. I knew it had to have taken a lot of time, effort, and loss of sleep on her part.

For me, that was authentic Christian love at its finest!

God worked mightily through my co-worker's prayerful obedience. As a result of those letters and conversations with my friend, I decided—out of sheer curiosity—to begin reading the Bible for myself. I wanted to know what it really said. My friend was eager to help me pick one out, and she encouraged me to begin with the Gospel of Matthew. So I did.

I decided to read six chapters every night before I fell asleep. I don't know why I decided on six chapters, but it seemed like a good number at the time. Even when I went to the bars and got drunk (usually two or three times a week), my plan was to return back to my dorm room and read the next six chapters before passing out. More often than not, I successfully made it through all six chapters.

Once, I even remember sitting at a bar with a beer in my hand, thinking, *I wish this place would hurry up and close so I can go home and read the Bible some more.*

How comforting it is to know that God's Word is so

wonderfully sharp that it can cut through the degeneracy of any mind. Even a highly intoxicated one.

During the weeks that followed, the Lord worked on me—pricking my conscience with the sharpness of His Word and cultivating the soil of my heart. One morning shortly thereafter, the Lord chose to call me into His kingdom.

SAVED BY GOD'S RADICAL LOVE

I went out drinking at one of the local nightclubs one night, got drunk, staggered back to my dorm room around three o'clock in the morning, read six chapters of the Bible, and then proceeded to pass out. Nothing much new there. Pretty typical stuff, I must say. However, the very next morning ushered in the dawn of my second birth.

I awoke in my bed around ten o'clock in the morning, smelling like a discarded cigarette and hung over with a slight headache. The curtains were drawn closed, but there was a single beam of sunshine poking through a crack in my window. While lying on my bed, I stared at the light beam's shape for some ten minutes. All of my attention was fixed on the light. It was just a normal ray of light, but as I examined its outline in the shadows of my room, I couldn't think of anything else except this verse from the Bible which I had recently read: "The Light shines in the darkness, and the darkness did not comprehend it."[256]

That verse rattled me.

It was at that very moment when I realized at I couldn't comprehend "the Light." I suddenly became appalled at

---

256 John 1:5

the wickedness of my sin. The Lord unmasked my ignorance, showing me the darkness of my soul and the ugliness of my spiritual condition. He revealed to me that I was in the darkness—no, I *was* the darkness—and that there was no light in me.

Not even a weak flicker.

I then began examining the contents of my room: the posters hanging on the walls, the music I listened to, the movies I watched, the clothes I wore, and everything else that defined who I was. I was ashamed and so convicted of my sin in the light of God's goodness that I began to sob.

The Lord yanked the veil from my blind eyes, revealing that unless He shined the light of His forgiveness in me, I would go to Hell forever. And rightly so. I was so convinced that everything about me offended God that I began to tremble. The evidence was too overwhelming.

I jumped out of bed and fell to my knees in tearful confession of sin. Begging for God's mercy, I repeatedly beat my chest because I remembered reading somewhere in the Bible that a sinner did that, and Jesus said he went away forgiven.[257]

I started naming every sin I could think of or remember having committed (yes, it was a long prayer). Ashamed because everything about my life offended my Creator, I prayed fervently for close to an hour. I ended that morning with glorious thanksgiving to my new Lord and Savior. A compassionate and relentless God had freed me from the bondage of sin. I knew that—without a doubt—I was eternally forgiven.

---

257 See Luke 18:9-14

Rising from my knees, I tore the posters off the wall and threw them into the trash, along with all my CDs, videos, and every possession I had which I felt didn't honor my new Lord. I didn't have many trinkets left over when I was finished, but I couldn't care less. All I wanted to do at that moment was to honor God's love for me.

Sin had become exceedingly sinful.

I then showered and walked to the cafeteria where I was supposed to meet my friends for lunch. They were the same guys I went out partying with the night before. I wanted to share my new faith with them, hoping they would appreciate my reason for not going out to the bars anymore.

MY FRIENDS' REACTION TO GOD'S RADICAL LOVE

I must confess that in my newfound joy, I never stopped to consider how ridiculous all of this was going to sound to my soon-to-be-ex-drinking buddies. All I thought about was how free I felt, and I wanted to share it with everyone I knew.

As you might suspect, my news didn't exactly fall on receptive ears. Half-intoxicated ears, yes, but not receptive.

My friends blasphemed, laughed, blasphemed, called me a hypocrite, blasphemed, and one of them even got rather belligerent. With spitting anger, he raised his voice and declared, "My father is a Lutheran pastor, and that practically guarantees me a front row seat in Heaven!"

Well, being just a babe in Christ, I didn't know how to respond to that. I tried to explain what happened to me, letting them know that God could save them as well...if they were willing. It didn't go over too well (humanly speaking, of course), but I had—unknowingly at the time—planted three new seeds.

GOD'S WILL FOR YOUR LIFE

Back then, I didn't think my first witnessing experience was all that successful. Today, however, I'm better informed. Christians sow the seed of the gospel, but the Lord must bring the increase. I had planted eternal seed, and that's precisely what two teenagers did for me when I was fifteen years old.

As I reflect upon those three witnessing experiences, I now understand that I was trying to duplicate with my ex-drinking buddies what someone had done for me. Intentionally loving other people, sharing the everlasting good news, and making followers of Jesus Christ is precisely that. Christians make disciples with the prayerful outcome of spiritual duplication. Believers share the good news with sinners, hoping to win souls for Christ, knowing that we—ourselves—were saved by similar means.

If God's children would simply get serious about the command of Great Commission Discipleship, the Lord would reveal His will for their lives. He'll use them to accomplish His work.

Actually, He will use *you* to accomplish His work.

In case you haven't figured it out by now, it is the reason you are still inhaling and exhaling right now. It is God's revealed will for your life today.